Mark
Twain &
the
Community

A UNIVERSITY OF
KENTUCKY STUDY

Mark Twain & the Community

Thomas Blues

THE UNIVERSITY PRESS OF KENTUCKY

Standard Book Number 8131-1201-X
Library of Congress Catalog Card Number 73-94063

for Kay

Contents

Preface

IN THIS essay I attempt to demonstrate how Mark Twain's complex attitudes toward the relation of the individual to the community influence the meaning and direction of his fiction. My fundamental argument is that at the center of Mark Twain's consciousness as a novelist was a vision of an idealized relation between the individual and the community, in which an independent individual could freely challenge the community's values, disrupt its sense of order, and yet somehow retain his identity as a conventional member of it. An impossible ideal, no doubt, and fraught with tensions that Mark Twain could not ultimately control; yet it underlies the structures and themes of each novel he wrote up to and including *Adventures of Huckleberry Finn.* It also exercised a compelling influence on the book that has lately been treated as the most important novel in the Mark Twain canon, *A Connecticut Yankee in King Arthur's Court.*

Recent criticism has rightly pointed out that to understand the nature of *A Connecticut Yankee*'s failure is to deepen our knowledge of Mark Twain's literary career—what sustained him as a writer of viable fiction before, what contributed to the decline of his powers in the works following it. The most influential argument is Henry Nash Smith's; in his view Hank Morgan's experience revealed to Mark Twain that "vernacular" values could not survive in an industrial society. The result, according to Smith, was a loss of faith in that society's value system and a crippling effect on his creative imagination.

But, as I shall argue, *A Connecticut Yankee* fails because Mark Twain could no longer effect the stratagem central to the structural coherence of each of his previous novels, his protagonist's commitment to the community whose values and stability he paradoxically repudiates. In chapter one I examine the novels of the 1870's and 1880's—*The Gilded Age, The Adventures of Tom Sawyer, The Prince and The Pauper,* and *Adventures of Huckleberry Finn*—to show that Mark Twain was deeply distrustful of the character and fearful for the fate of the individual who attempts to triumph over the community. In each of these novels he contrived compromise resolutions to grant his protagonists victories over the community without alienating them from it, so reluctant was he to project a character into the moral isolation that in his mind independence necessarily implied. But in his fifth novel Mark Twain, for a complex of reasons, could not effect a similar easy resolution.

Chapter two is a detailed examination of *A Connecticut Yankee.* I begin by tracing through the journalistic writings of the 1860's and 1870's the prototypes of Hank Morgan—strong, aggressive personalities who dominated the community in the interests of moral and material progress—in order to demonstrate that Mark Twain's skepticism of the independent individual conflicts with the assumptions that his Yankee represents. In the development of Hank Morgan, I will argue, Mark Twain faced the fact that the individual is in no sense the superior of the community he triumphs over—ostensibly in its best interests—and that the community, on the other hand, is an unworthy refuge for the individual.

But, in recognizing these tragic truths Mark Twain was not reconciled to the breakdown of the ideal relation he had so heavily relied upon, a fact which accounts not only for the total collapse of *A Connecticut Yankee,* but also in large part for the bitter, cynical fiction of the last two decades of his life. My final chapter, therefore, attempts to show how the loss of the sense of a meaningful relation between individual and community affects his late fiction.

Difficult as it is to define precisely, the term *community* as I apply it to this study should be explained. Early and late, Mark Twain instinctively chose small towns as settings in his fiction. Even in his late fiction, when he vilified society at large ("the damned human race") he tended to objectify the target of his criticism as the town. St. Petersburg, Dawson's Landing, Camelot, Hadleyburg, Eseldorf—these towns are more than mere geographical or political loci; they exist as social entities (defined by their embodiment of a complex cluster of official values and attitudes) and serve to subsume their individual inhabitants into a collective role of opponent, conscience, and audience for Mark Twain's protagonists. It is in the attempt to evoke this sense of the town as social organism operating as fictional antagonist that I use the term.

I am indebted to a number of people who have helped me with this project since its beginning: John C. Gerber, Clark Griffith, and especially Paul Baender, to whose critical and editorial intelligence I owe much. Martin Dillon, Joseph Gardner, Robert Hemenway, and Thomas Stroup—friends and colleagues at the University of Kentucky—took the time to read and criticize the manuscript at various stages of its composition. This may have been a better book had I adopted more of their suggestions, and I must assume full responsibility for errors of fact and deficiencies of judgment. I wish to thank the Kentucky Research Foundation for summer research fellowships that enabled me to work on this project and *Modern Fiction Studies* for permission to use in this book material published in that journal in somewhat different form. Finally, I am particularly grateful for the Mark Twain criticism of Henry Nash Smith. Here and there I take issue with his interpretations of Mark Twain's writings, fully aware that without them this book could not have been written.

CHAPTER ONE

The Strategy of Compromise

THE central characters of the four novels written prior to *A Connecticut Yankee*—*The Gilded Age* (1873), *The Adventures of Tom Sawyer* (1876), *The Prince and The Pauper* (1882), and *Adventures of Huckleberry Finn* (1885)—attempt to triumph over the community, endangering in the process not only its welfare but their own as well. This is not to suggest, however, that Mark Twain was unsympathetic to his protagonists, whose efforts connote wit, daring, and a healthy urge to free oneself from the community's restrictions. But each novel reveals Mark Twain's concerned awareness that self-realization at the expense of the community's stability causes moral as well as physical isolation from it. The crucial fact is that the central figure in each novel, consciously or unconsciously, harbors an aggressive design against the community: Colonel Sellers is deeply involved in criminal schemes; Tom Sawyer exercises his pirate fantasies against an entire town; Tom Canty poses as a prince and almost usurps the English throne; Huck Finn, more passive than his predecessors, nevertheless frees a slave as prelude to a planned career of "wickedness." But Mark Twain was reluctant to cast his sympathetic characters beyond the protective fold of the community. In each novel he provided his hero with a victory over the community that in no way endangered his relations with it, a compromise resolution that permitted triumph without alienation.

M ARK Twain avoided a direct confrontation between Colonel Sellers and the community by allowing him to bypass it completely in the pursuit of his dreams. The Colonel would appear to be the perfect symbol of the corrupt values that Mark Twain and his collaborator, Charles Dudley Warner, satirize in *The Gilded Age*. He guarantees easy wealth to gullible believers, but his unfilled promises cause their ruin. His grandiose plans— officially linked to material progress and human betterment—are really elaborate devices to loot the public treasury. But the sordid actualities of the Gilded Age are alien to the spirit and scope of Sellers's imagination. He enjoys his triumphs in a world of his own creation while others must assume responsibility for the harm he generates.

Sellers's magnificent visions are matched only by the power of his spellbinding rhetoric. His tongue "was a magician's wand that turned dried apples into figs and water into wine as easily as it could change a hovel into a palace and present poverty into imminent future riches."[1] His persuasive power leads Squire Hawkins deep into poverty and turns his son into a wasted dreamer of riches. But the Colonel is not held responsible by those who know him best. " 'He's an honest soul,' " the Squire's wife testifies, " 'and means the very best in the world. . . . He has splendid ideas, and he'll divide his chances with his friends with a free hand, the good generous soul'" (V, 10–11). She attributes his failures to an indefinite "something [that] does seem to always interfere and spoil everything'" (V, 11).

What spoils everything is precisely what saves the "honest soul" from responsibility, the fact that for Sellers the world of his imagination is the only reality he knows. To contrast the Colonel to Senator Dilworthy, the book's chief villain, is to see the critical differences between one who makes appearance his reality and one who flourishes by exploiting the discrepancy. Dilworthy, a hypocritical grafter, is one of the most powerful men in the Senate. In one day he addresses a Sunday school class on the necessity of integrity in public life and bribes a state legislator to insure his reelection. Because he knows how to succeed in the corrupt world Dilworthy is a rich man. But Sellers not only hasn't a dime to his name, he doesn't need the money; his imagination more than supplies his needs. In the novel's most famous scene the Colonel plays lordly host in his humble shack, serving up raw turnips and water as if they were a gourmet's delight: "'Lord bless me, I go in for having the best of a thing, even if it does cost a little more—it's the best economy in the long run. These are the Early Malcolm—it's a turnip that can't be produced except in just one orchard, and the supply never is up to the demand. Take some more water . . . you can't drink too much water with fruit—all the doctors say that'" (V, 107–108).

This difference between the Senator and the Colonel is important because it allowed Mark Twain to cast Dilworthy as the morally culpable villain and preserve Sellers as a harmless but triumphant visionary. It is Sellers, for example, who conceives the extraordinary plan of con-

verting a creekside settlement some fifty miles from the
Missouri River into a thriving river port and rail center.
It is Dilworthy who uses the scheme as a vehicle to
defraud the public. Viewing the wilderness, Sellers
enjoys his vision of a civilized and progressive community, complete with courthouse, churches, and the
" 'University up there, on rising ground' " (V, 172).
Dilworthy sees only a chance to push through a con-
gressional appropriation to line his and other grafters'
pockets. Again, as representative of Laura and Washington Hawkins, Sellers must share in the final responsibility for the nefarious Tennessee Land Bill, a grand
design to sell the Hawkins landholdings to the federal
government for the alleged purpose of building a Negro
university on them. Dilworthy is the prime mover
behind the project, however, and when he is exposed
as an election rigger the bill is defeated in Congress.

Young Washington Hawkins, broken in spirit and
health as a result of the failure, becomes an old man
overnight. But the older man, whose plans have included
the perfection of a perpetual-motion machine, cannot
be deeply touched by real disaster. Unaffected by failure
or guilt, by a sense of his own life in time, Sellers vows
to study law and start a new career. " 'There's worlds
of money in it!—whole worlds of money! . . . Climb,
and climb, and climb—and wind up on the Supreme
bench. Beriah Sellers, Chief Justice of the Supreme
Court of the United States, sir! A made man for all
time and eternity! That's the way *I* block it out sir—and
it's clear as day—clear as the rosy morn!' " (VI, 307–308).

The Colonel is undefeated because the real world
of fraud, greed, failure, and disillusionment is irrelevant
to his imagination. Because he so totally inhabits a
fantasy world, he avoids moral responsibility for the
corrupt values he officially represents.

THE conflict between the individual and the community is more sharply defined and ingeniously resolved in Mark Twain's second novel. If in *The Gilded Age* he could protect the Colonel by permitting him to live in a fantasy world while a scapegoat did the dirty work in the real one, Mark Twain could not apply that solution to *Tom Sawyer*. For Tom not only wants to make his dreams come true in the real world, he wants to be applauded by the adult community for violating its stability.

Walter Blair has argued that Tom Sawyer is "a working out in fictional form of a boy's maturing." He bases his thesis on the supposition that "every subplot in the book eventuates in an expression of adult approval."[2] But Tom's triumphs are made possible by Mark Twain's transformation of an adult community into one very much resembling a world of children. In granting Tom his triumphs without endangering either the town or his standing in it, Mark Twain furnished him with a community that applauded its victimizer and was more than willing to regard victimization as a virtue.

The novel early provides two important indicators of Tom's notion of a dominant relation to the adult community and of Mark Twain's method of protecting him from the consequences of its realization. The first, Tom's pirate fantasy, should be treated as an expression of genuine aggression. Although he has no serious intentions of terrorizing St. Petersburg by main force, he gains by fraud and guile the quality of submission he desires in his daydream: "he would suddenly appear at the old village and stalk into church, brown and weather-beaten, in his black velvet doublet and trunks, his great jack-boots, his crimson sash, his belt bristling with horse-pistols, his crime-rusted cutlass at his side, his slouch hat with waving plumes, his black flag un-furled, with the skull and cross-bones on it, and hear with swelling ecstasy the whisperings, 'it's Tom Sawyer the Pirate!—the Black Avenger of the Spanish Main!'" (VIII, 75). As Tom strives to realize his dream he risks alienating himself from the town, but Mark Twain reduces the adult world to make his performances seem innocent and entertaining diversions.

The second indicator, the famous whitewashing scene, is a capsule demonstration of how Mark Twain reshapes the community to fit Tom's imaginative dimensions of it. The scene begins with Aunt Polly vowing to turn Tom's "Saturday holiday into captivity at hard labor" (VIII, 11). Tom quickly abandons self-pity and beguiles the "free boys" into paying him for the privilege of painting the fence. But Aunt Polly is the most important link in his chain of victims. Impressed with what she sup-poses is his diligence, she gives him an apple and a "lecture upon the added value and flavor a treat took to itself when it came without sin through virtuous effort" (VIII, 21).

Little is at stake in the whitewashing episode, but the pattern of Tom's first triumph is repeated on a more serious scale in the flight to Jackson's Island and back. For Tom returns to convince an entire adult community that a cruel hoax is fun and to persuade Aunt Polly that it is actually a virtuous act. The Black Avenger and his friends find that leaving town is one thing, breaking with it something else. After the initial excite-ment of camping out and watching the townspeople search for their bodies had worn off, the boys "could not keep back thoughts of certain persons at home who were not enjoying this fine frolic as much as they were" (VIII, 127). Anxious to remain on the island and at the same time maintain a conscience-clear relationship with his home, Tom returns at night to leave a reassuring note; it reads, " '*We ain't dead—we are only off being pirates*' " (VIII, 158). From a hiding place in his house Tom listens to the conversation and "was sufficiently touched by his aunt's grief to long to rush out from under the bed and overwhelm her with joy—and the theatrical gorgeousness of the thing appealed strongly to his nature,' too, but he resisted and lay still" (VIII, 132). Tom learns that the funeral will be held the following Sunday—four days hence—and when Aunt Polly goes to bed he almost leaves the note. "His heart was full of pity for her. He took out his sycamore scroll and placed it by the candle. But something occurred to him, and he lingered considering. His face lighted with a happy solution of his thought; he put the bark hastily in his pocket" (VIII, 133). Tom's victory over conscience clears the way for his sensational return to the town.

Actually, his intention to appear alive at his own funeral serves two purposes. Next day on Jackson's Island Tom staves off mutiny by promising his homesick gang a glorious return if they will hold out for a few more days. Having won his boys over, Tom completes his triumph on a larger scale in St. Petersburg three days later. True to his pirate fantasy Tom returns to a crowded church. The minister urges the startled assembly into a hymn of joyful thanksgiving, and "As the 'sold' congregation trooped out they said they would almost be willing to be made ridiculous again to hear Old Hundred sung like that once more" (VIII, 153).

Aunt Polly is not so readily won over; she does not think it was such " 'a fine joke . . . to keep everybody suffering 'most a week' " (VIII, 154). But her hesitancy is grist for Tom's mill. First he tells his aunt he returned in a dream to console her. When that story is exposed he tells her of his actual return, of the suppressed note,

and a half-truth about the purpose of the clandestine
visit: " 'I wanted to keep you from grieving—that was
all that made me come' " (VIII, 167). She accepts the
story as a forgivable lie—" 'it was such good-heartedness
in him to tell it' "—and when she finds the note in Tom's
jacket she vows she " 'could forgive the boy, now, if he'd
committed a million sins!' " (VIII, 168–69). Her sentimentality leads her to obscure a sterner truth. Anxious
to believe in Tom's essential virtue, Aunt Polly finds it
in a cruel and deliberate hoax.

Aunt Polly's emotional excess, however, is typical of
that of the adult community at large. Albert E. Stone
says that Tom is essentially a passive character "sub-
servient in the main to the adult schedule of events,"[3]
but he fails to consider that Tom's triumphs over the
community are possible only because he can depend
upon its hysterical and childish reactions to his antics.
The Jackson's Island hoax is but the first of four episodes
in which the townspeople demonstrate their inability
to distinguish between a genuinely heroic action and a
vulgar bid for the limelight. Nor can they react to
either except with sensational emotional display.

Tom's return from the island reinvolves him in an
unsettled moral problem—his silence in the face of Muff
Potter's certain conviction for a crime he did not commit.
Having witnessed Injun Joe's murder of Dr. Robinson,
Tom and Huck Finn vowed silence for fear of the half-
breed's reprisal. Tom's conscience increasingly nags him
as the trial date draws closer, but he manages to live
with his guilt until he can reveal the truth to a packed
courtroom. One remembers that Tom had earlier hesi-
tated until the most dramatic moment to take Becky
Thatcher's punishment for a ripped anatomy book and
that she had praised his nobility; now an even more
startling revelation captures a larger adoration. The

courtroom audience "hung upon his words, taking no note of time, rapt in the ghastly fascinations of the tale" (VIII, 197). His story makes Tom "a glittering hero once more—the pet of the old, the envy of the young" (VIII, 198). The fact that Muff Potter has waited in agony for months to hang for a crime he is innocent of is forgotten.

When Tom returns from the dead a second time, after his ordeal with Becky Thatcher in the cave, the town enjoys not a moment of quiet thankfulness but a gaudy parade: "the population massed itself and moved toward the river, met the children coming in an open carriage drawn by shouting citizens, thronged around it, joined its homeward march, and swept magnificently up the main street roaring huzzah after huzzah!" (VIII, 263–64). Tom's final triumph is his dramatic display of the treasure to the citizens assembled to honor Huck Finn. This last sensation steals the scene from Huck and nearly enervates the town: "It was talked about, gloated over, glorified, until the reason of many of the citizens tottered under the strain of the unhealthy excitement" (VIII, 285).

At the end of the novel Tom successfully persuades Huck Finn to return to the Widow Douglas's home. His argument is that respectability and new wealth "'ain't going to keep me back from turning robber'" (VIII, 289). Professor Blair views this as the culmination of Tom's growing up, his capitulation to the "enemy."[4] But in fact the opposite is true. Tom's claim that he can at once maintain membership in the respectable adult community and continue his career as its victimizer is valid precisely because the town has never failed to come over to his side. Mark Twain provides Tom Sawyer with a community which willingly capitulates to his selfish desires for awed and reverent attention, a community which reacts with excessive benevolence to whatever he does. Though his depredations are potentially destructive, no permanent harm ever comes to those who bear the burden of his imagination.

IN HIS next novel Mark Twain again arranges his boy-hero's triumph over the community without causing his alienation from it. But in an important sense *The Prince and The Pauper* begins where *Tom Sawyer* leaves off. In this book about a beggar who nearly becomes king of England Mark Twain focuses attention upon an issue barely touched upon in *Tom Sawyer*—the responsibility that comes with power over the community. At the end of that book Tom has become, with Huck, a hero of mighty proportion, even, in a sense, king of the village: "Wherever Tom and Huck appeared they were courted, admired, stared at. The boys were not able to remember that their remarks had possessed weight before; but now their sayings were treasured and repeated; everything they did seemed somehow to be regarded as remarkable; they had evidently lost the power of doing and saying commonplace things. . . . The village paper published biographical sketches of the boys" (VIII, 285). With only one exception—when he is exposed as a fraudulent biblical scholar in Sunday school—Tom never has to face the consequences of the attention he calls to himself. Momentary embarrassment is the price Tom pays for this particular Pyrrhic victory; Mark Twain passes over the incident and it is swiftly forgotten. But in the story of the boy usurper Mark Twain shows that falsely gained power is a betrayal of the community and that the price one pays is disillusionment and moral isolation.

Like Tom Sawyer, Tom Canty wants to escape the

restraints of an oppressive situation—a vicious father and a London slum. In the beginning his form of escape is fantasy, "delicious picturings to himself of the charmed life of a petted prince in a regal palace" (XI, 5). The fantasy has such control over him that he begins imitating the gestures and speech of royalty in the presence of his Offal Court neighbors. Their mockery makes his life even more miserable, until his dream becomes a reality. The exact double of Prince Edward, he is one day invited into the palace and ordered by the Prince to exchange clothes with him. Edward is subsequently thrown into the streets by guards who mistake him for the young beggar.

Tom's first response is similar to Tom Sawyer's initial reaction to Aunt Polly's punishment—regret for his lost freedom. Like his predecessor, however, Tom Canty soon adjusts to his role in the spotlight and happily anticipates his coronation as Edward VI. But despite the fact that what little we see of Tom's administration is merciful and just, Mark Twain mocks his pretensions and characterizes him as a self-conscious imposter who cannot lose his outsider's point of view. Significantly, Tom cannot locate the Great Seal for his worried minions. He has used the strange, heavy instrument as a nutcracker, but he cannot associate it with its official purpose.

As Tom rides in parade through the streets toward Westminster Abbey and his coronation, he wishes his Offal Court friends "could recognize him, and realize that the derided mock king of the slums and back alleys was become a real king, with illustrious dukes and princes for his humble menials, and the English world at his feet" (XI, 239). But when his mother recognizes him he denies her. As Professor Regan has pointed out, Tom's moral failure clearly indicates that "life in the court . . . can corrupt even the purest, the most innocent will."[5] Despite the fact that he might have been a humane and intelligent monarch he could not have maintained the throne conscious of his essentially fraudulent position. In the face of his own denial Tom's guilt and fear return full force; he prays again to be "'free of my captivity!'" (XI, 242). The dream of glory, once realized, turns out to be solitary confinement in a moral prison.

Mark Twain extricated Tom Canty from his dilemma by using the real king as one part of an interchangeable identity. Without this device Tom could not have ultimately gained what Mark Twain's boys must—the reward without the moral consequence of triumph. For not only does his inadvertent substitution for the Prince provide Tom with a throne, Edward—who of course has rightful power—returns to relieve him of its burden, restore him to the community, and provide him with a permanent and morally acceptable triumph over it. This exchange of identity is a refinement of the Sellers-Dilworthy shuffle, in which the Senator takes all the responsibility while the Colonel remains untouched by his corrupt involvements. Tom is given charge of Christ's Hospital, a charitable institution for the poor, along with a fancy title. "As long as he lasted he was honored . . . wherever he appeared the crowd fell apart, making way for him, and whispering, one to another, 'Doff thy hat, it is the King's Ward'" (XI, 273). Like Tom Sawyer, Tom Canty in the end becomes King without really having to be a king.

As for the real Edward, his career as street urchin underlines Mark Twain's insistence upon the individual's need for a conscience-free relation to the community. What attracts the Prince to the ragged Tom is what makes Huck Finn the envy of all the respectable boys in *Tom Sawyer:* " 'If that I could but clothe me in raiment like to thine, and strip my feet, and revel in the mud once, just once, with none to rebuke me or forbid, meseemeth I could forego the crown!' " (XI, 16). Of course he has no such permanent desire, but his sojourn in the world serves both himself and his people well. Unlike Tom Canty's rise to power, which isolates him from the community, the young Prince's travails bring him closer to it.

If at the outset he longs for the freedom of mud and rags, at the end of his travels he is more than ready to reassume his authority with an understanding and compassion that only his experience among the poor and oppressed could have made possible. Edward learns that poverty, suffering, and even criminal behavior are often the direct result of the brutality of English law as it is written and administered. He sees clearly that the government has not humanely exercised its responsibility to the people. The Prince vows to one victim that " 'the laws that have dishonored thee, and shamed the English name, shall be swept from the statute-books. The world is made wrong, kings should go to school to their own laws at times, and so learn mercy' " (XI, 224). A result of the Prince's education, Mark Twain concludes, is that "the reign of Edward VI. was a singularly merciful one for those harsh times" (XI, 274). Power, informed with humanity, is Edward's link with the community.

EDWARD's sense of his relation to the community, stemming as it does from his exposure to it during his masquerade, constitutes part of an important difference between the young King and Huck Finn. Edward must endure experiences not unlike Huck's—the brutality of a degenerate "father," the intimidation of the mob, the uneasy company of outlaws. But he has a place to return to, and his journey makes him both qualified and anxious to take his rightful place in society. Huck's journey teaches him that he has no place in society, that only as an outlaw from it can he be true to himself. Because of this reversal, *Adventures of Huckleberry Finn* was at once Mark Twain's greatest achievement and, in a sense, his biggest failure.

Huck Finn, unlike the two Toms, has no particular desire at the beginning of his book to initiate action, control anyone, or reshape the world to suit himself. If his basic instinct is to shrink from civilization's restraints, he demonstrates no intention to flee the respectable community. After four months in the Widow Douglas's home, under a regime that stresses cleanliness of mind and body in addition to book-learning, Huck finds he "was sort of getting used to the widow's ways. . . . I liked the old ways best, but I was getting so I liked the new ones, too, a little bit" (XIII, 21). When he is kidnapped by his drunken father he is content also to live in a wilderness hovel until Pap's brutality forces him to flee for fear of his life.

Basic to Huck's character, and a complement to his essential passivity, is his instinctive feeling that any action, whether on his or anyone else's part, is likely to have a harmful effect. When he first went to live in her house, "the widow she cried over me, and called me a poor lost lamb . . . but she never meant no harm by it" (XIII, 2). Miss Watson "told me all about the bad place . . . I said I wished I was there. She got mad then, but I didn't mean no harm" (XIII, 3). This special sensitivity puts him always on the defensive, makes him hesitate to initiate action for fear of the consequences. It leads him to exaggerate his role in precipitating the final slaughter in the Grangerford-Sheperdson feud and to quietly endure the intimidation of the King and the Duke on the raft.

More important is the fact that Huck accepts the viewpoints of the respectable community, retaining even in flight its moral and emotional values and even its tastes. When he and Jim steal food they call it "borrowing"; he is impressed with the Grangerford parlor and ventures the opinion that Emmeline's verse was "very good"; he is as quick as the rest of the townspeople in the rush to watch Boggs die (XIII, 91, 138–42, 199). Sharing the community's view of himself as low-down and no-account, he also accepts the attitude toward slavery that belongs to the society from which he shelters a runaway Negro: "Here was this nigger, which I had as good as helped to run away, coming right out flat-footed and saying he would steal his children—children that belonged to a man I didn't even know; a man that hadn't ever done me no harm" (XIII, 123–24).

Because of his passivity and his tendency to make moral judgments from the community's perspective, Huck, though in retreat, never asserts himself against its moral codes. Not, at any rate, until a point is reached where his method of passive retreat is no longer applicable to a specific situation, where there is nobody to tell a lie to. He must finally make a choice between continuing the journey alone or taking action against the culture he flees from and at the same time feels morally responsible to. Unwilling to harm anyone, he is trapped by his bond of friendship to Jim and his moral obligation—as he views it—to Miss Watson and society's code.

Twice he preserves Jim's freedom, and twice he states his belief that in doing so he betrays his rightful owner.

The first time he thinks, " 'What had poor Miss Watson done to you that you could see her nigger go off right under your eyes and never say one single word?' " (XIII, 123). But there is a significant difference between the first decision and the second. The first time he saves Jim he reacts in immediate response to a specific crisis. Although the second decision is also prompted by crisis, Huck has ample time to think out his alternatives, which implies the necessity of making a policy decision. Since he decides not to notify Miss Watson of Jim's whereabouts, he feels he must rescue him from his confinement. The latter alternative, Huck knows, is an aggressive act against the community, an act he equates with damnation. Yet he is unable to harden his heart against the slave who has become his friend. His decision to go to hell is also a conscious commitment to outlawry: "I would take up wickedness again, which was in my line, being brung up to it. . . . And for a starter I would go to work and steal Jim out of slavery again; and if I could think up anything worse, I would do that, too; because as long as I was in, and in for good, I might as well go the whole hog" (XIII, 297).

Huck proceeds to the Phelps farm to carry out his dark commitment, but the Phelpses mistake him for their nephew, Tom Sawyer, whose arrival they have been expecting. Tom, when he arrives, decides to perpetuate the deception that his aunt and uncle unwittingly initiated; he poses as his brother Sid while Huck continues as Tom. Huck is amazed that Tom wants to participate in Jim's rescue, but he accepts Tom's cooperation and his leadership. At the end of a broadly farcical "evasion" episode that Tom controls, he informs a gathered community that Jim was free all the time; on her deathbed Miss Watson has released him from slavery.

Henry Nash Smith argues persuasively that the shift in tone and point of view through the last twelve chapters of *Huckleberry Finn,* in which the clowning of Tom Sawyer effectively erases the simple dignity of Huck, is to be accounted for in terms of Mark Twain's recognition that "Huck's and Jim's journey down the river could not be imagined as leading to freedom for either of them."[6] Smith claims that Tom's dominance in the book's final section, and Mark Twain's partial identification of himself with Tom, "was one response to his recognition that Huck's and Jim's quest for freedom was only a dream."[7]

I suggest an alternative view—that the dream did not run its course, but that Mark Twain deliberately returned Huck Finn to the community before irreparably isolating him from it. As we have seen, Mark Twain had never failed in his novels to permit his boy-heroes to triumph over the community while retaining membership in it, that is, to indulge their selfish desires without doing the community any harm. Huck's river journey, as long as it lasts, permits him to flee the community without directly rebelling against its values. And as long as Huck can judge himself from the community's viewpoint, he may retain his ties. But when he decides to act against the community he commits himself to its betrayal, an important step beyond passive flight.

It is enlightening to compare Huck's decision to rescue the slave Jim from the Phelps farm with Tom's to free the pariah Muff Potter from an unjust death sentence. However delayed, however motivated by selfishness, Tom's decision was obviously right. Moreover, his revelation brought him closer to the community, earning him its admiration. Huck's decision, once set into action on behalf of a real slave, would have cast him beyond the community, a moral outcast past redemption. This Mark Twain was reluctant to allow; therefore, he set in motion elaborate machinery to restore Huck to the community and at the same time preserve his moral victory over it.

Huck makes his decision in chapter 31, and it is clear that it weighs heavily upon him as he approaches the Phelps farm at the beginning of chapter 32. "When I got there it was all still and Sunday-like, and hot and sunshiny; the hands was gone to the fields; and there was them kind of faint dronings of bugs and flies in the air that makes it seem so lonesome and like everybody's dead and gone; and if a breeze fans along and quivers the leaves it makes you feel mournful, because you feel like it's spirits whispering—spirits that's been dead ever so many years—and you always think they're talking about *you*. As a general thing it makes a body wish *he* was dead, too, and done with it all" (XIII, 303). Dispirited, isolated, and lonesome as he moves toward his goal, burdened by the awful weight of conscience, he soon has cause to rejoice. Sally and Silas Phelps mistake him for their nephew, and at the end of the chapter that begins so mournfully, Huck says, "it was like being born again, I was so glad to find out who I was. . . . Being Tom Sawyer was easy and comfortable" (XIII, 310). Huck's delight must have been shared by Mark Twain, for he had bridged a crisis very similar to one he had faced in the writing of *Tom Sawyer*.

Hamlin Hill's examination of Mark Twain's *Tom Sawyer* manuscript shows that midway through its composition he faced a crucial decision that determined the course of the remainder of the novel. On the manuscript's first page Mark Twain indicated his intention to send Tom on his travels; he would fight " 'the Battle of Life in many lands' " and return to the town as a middle-aged adult.[8] Jackson's Island would have been the logical point of departure, and certain residual material in the published book suggests that Mark Twain had so considered it. Tom writes two notes before he embarks on his clandestine visit to St. Petersburg. One he leaves in Joe Harper's hat, along with his "school-boy treasures" (VIII, 128). Its contents are not fully revealed, but the note is clearly a kind of will, leaving the "treasures" to the gang if Tom does not return to the island by breakfast-time (VIII, 134–35). We know what the note to Aunt Polly says, but its contents are not disclosed until after the funeral episode. Hill shows that Mark Twain himself was not certain whether the note would contain Tom's farewell to his aunt or set up his return to the town.[9] Mark Twain's immediate reaction to the problem was to cease work on the book, but when he returned to it he "chose not to have Tom start his travels."[10] Without doubt the resolution of the crisis, which crucially affects plot and theme, also lifts a temporarily gloomy tone. Just before Tom writes his notes he and his gang are afflicted by homesickness and guilt. But Tom's return to the island and his announced plan for the gang's reentry into civilization set off a joyful celebration (VIII, 140).

Though I cannot produce evidence corresponding to Hill's manuscript discoveries, I submit that Mark Twain faced and similarly resolved an identical problem in chapter 32 of *Huckleberry Finn*. In *Tom Sawyer* Mark Twain prevented Tom from beginning his travels; now he prevented Huck from continuing his. Mark Twain had sent Tom back to the community to triumph over it. Later, with the reintroduction of Tom Sawyer, he did precisely the same for Huck. For Tom's return to *Huckleberry Finn* provided Mark Twain with two devices

he had previously used to guarantee his boy-heroes'
triumphs over the community and to save them from
moral outlawry.

Tom Sawyer's letter to Aunt Polly had been delayed
but ultimately delivered. Huck's letter to Miss Watson,
notifying her of Jim's whereabouts and of his own
fidelity to society's angle of vision, was torn up. Still,
the message got through. More awkwardly, but for the
same reason he initiated it in *The Prince and The Pauper,*
Mark Twain brought back with Tom Sawyer a variation
on the interchangeable identity. Though he poses as his
brother Sid, Tom actually takes over Huck's duty to
free Jim, while Huck becomes Tom Sawyer. And as
Huck himself says, it is inconceivable that respectable
Tom Sawyer could ever be a "*nigger-stealer*" (XIII, 314).
In becoming Tom, Huck's problem is only partly solved,
but Tom's news from St. Petersburg, that a dying Miss
Watson had long since freed Jim, completely lifts Huck's
burden. Miss Watson's action seems implausible because
she reverses the values of a community in which she
has been a conventional figure.[11] But Mark Twain
needed this reversal because it rendered Huck's rebellion against the community pointless and harmless.
We have seen this device on a larger scale in *Tom Sawyer.*
There the transformation of the adult community permits Tom to become a pirate without leaving town.
Now, in a similar way, the adult community has been
transformed to grant Huck his triumph over it without
really threatening it. Huck made a great decision without knowing he was agonizing over the fate of a free
man. Had Huck's decision to rescue Jim been carried
out under the same circumstances which necessitated
it, Huck could have achieved a genuine triumph over
the community. But although Mark Twain wanted to
grant his protagonist this victory, he was deeply afraid

of the risks. Therefore, he utilized the machinery of compromise to prevent Huck's moral alienation from the community and to provide him with an illusory triumph over it. Once Huck's freedom and his victory were in danger of becoming real, Mark Twain could not allow them to be true.

WE HAVE seen in the novels preceding *Huckleberry Finn* Mark Twain's distrust of and fear for the individual who sets himself apart from the community. He repeatedly makes it clear that his protagonists' efforts to triumph over it lead to isolation from it. It is evident that the desires of Colonel Sellers, Tom Sawyer, and Tom Canty are potentially harmful; we can understand why the boys' consciences attack them and why, subsequently, they are restored to the community. But why Mark Twain felt compelled to lift the burden of overt rebellion from Huck's shoulders is not so obvious and cannot be attributed solely to what Leo Marx says was a "failure of nerve."[12]

When Huck decides to free Jim he acts in opposition to his "acquired conscience," composed of values inimical to his more instinctively humane impulses.[13] A possibility is that Huck's break with this conscience raised Mark Twain's fear of what might happen to Huck as a result of his decision to go to hell. External and internal evidence suggest that Mark Twain deeply distrusted Huck's future as an outlaw, that he feared Huck might become an unprincipled pariah, similar, say, to his father.

At the end of the novel Huck vows to "light out for the territory," an irrelevant resolution because he may leave "civilization" as a member in good standing, not as a rebellious outcast. But earlier Pap Finn makes a

similar vow that precedes more serious consequences.
A deadbeat drunk, incapable of reform, Pap is in all
respects a degenerate outsider; yet he considers himself a member of the community. His tirade against a
"govment" that will steal a man's son and allow a
"nigger" to vote is a prelude to his resolve to disassociate
himself from it: " 'Says I, for two cents I'd leave the
blamed country and never come a-near it ag'in' " (XIII,
37). Violent death is all he could expect as a wastrel
beyond society's boundaries. More important, his dismal
life and death suggest what can happen to the individual
who sets himself apart from the community. Now, one
does not readily anticipate a like future for Huck, yet
such a future he himself sadly but philosophically accepts. He attempts to help the marooned criminals
aboard the *Walter Scott* because "I begun to think how
dreadful it was, even for murderers, to be in such a
fix. I says to myself, there ain't no telling but I might
come to be a murderer myself yet, and then how would
I like it?" (XIII, 100). When his efforts to arrange
rescue fail, Huck views their deaths with a sadness not
entirely blunted by the comic phrasing of his philosophical resignation: "I felt a little bit heavyhearted about
the gang, but not much, for I reckoned if they could
stand it I could" (XIII, 104). Of course, we are more
likely to view Huck's sympathy as further evidence of
his generous and humane spirit, but in light of his
overt decision to "take up wickedness" there is good
reason to take his remarks quite literally.

Mark Twain had earlier dealt with the theme of antisocial behavior resulting from freeing oneself from the
community's restrictions. In "The Facts Concerning the
Recent Carnival of Crime in Connecticut," written in
1876, he told the story of a middle-aged man who
captures and kills his conscience. A gnarled and

grotesque creature, the conscience explains his function
as follows: " 'I don't care *what* act you may turn your
hand to, I can straightway whisper a word in your ear
and make you think you have committed a dreadful
meanness. It is my *business*—and my joy—to make you
repent of *every*thing you do' " (XIX, 316–17). The
monstrous figure of conscience complements the narrator's more familiar nemesis, his Aunt Mary. Sweet,
lovable, and kindhearted, she can also be a torment with
her constant nagging to give up smoking and take up
good works. Though he is fond of her, the narrator
also knows that she is as much his enemy as the creature
he has imprisoned in his parlor. Thus, when he murders
his conscience he also turns upon the aunt: " 'Out . . .
with your paupers, your charities, your reforms, your
pestilent morals! You behold before you a man whose
life-conflict is done, whose soul is at peace; a man
whose heart is dead to sorrow, dead to suffering, dead
to remorse; a man WITHOUT A CONSCIENCE!' "
(XIX, 325). From that moment on the narrator's life
is unalloyed happiness. He gleefully confesses that
after the symbolic murder of conventional morality
he has committed wanton arson, swindled a helpless
widow, and murdered thirty-eight of his enemies (XIX,
325).

Comic hyperbole disguises a problem Mark Twain
treated more seriously if more furtively in *Huckleberry
Finn*. Possibly he feared that Huck's triumph over conventional conscience and his flight from civilization
might cause him to abandon himself completely to antisocial, even destructive behavior. Perhaps that is why
Mark Twain extricated Huck from the consequences of
his decision to free Jim and go to hell.

In this context, then, freedom must be viewed as a
potentially self-destructive burden. Why Mark Twain so

viewed it may be related to his own experience and consciousness of the American frontier. For it is to the frontier, the territory beyond organized human community, that Huck vows to flee. Charles Crowe sees Huck's flight toward freedom as an "alienating ordeal" and Huck as representative of "the archetypal American experience." He points out that "the abandonment of fathers, cultures, and sometimes native speech was not easy, and frequently men in their later years had to face the implications of history and society, abandoned selves and half-forgotten communities. To 'light out for the territory' really did mean freedom and fulfillment, but the pioneer-immigrant from Hannibal, Missouri, or Warsaw, Poland, had to undertake the voyage with a heavy burden of guilt. Those who 'deserted' and 'betrayed' ancient homelands sometimes paid the price of alienation in human coin, in a sense of *malaise* which was enhanced when the bright Western hope emerged in reality as the 'dark and bloody hunting ground' or the 'howling wilderness'. . . . The pioneer's march across the continent tended to create a contempt toward things which could end in a destructive contempt of self—if game existed for casual mass destruction, streams to be emptied of fish, soil for thoughtless exploitation . . . then it is not surprising that the violated land sometimes . . . reflected the rape of the continent."[14]

William Manierre views Huck's separations from society as forced, not willful, and distinguishes him from the frontiersman who willingly faces the isolation of the wilderness: "unlike Natty Bumppo, Huckleberry Finn does not like to be alone."[15] Finally, Leslie Fiedler thinks Huck is but potentially related to the Faustian outsiders of Melville and Hawthorne—Ahab, Pierre, Hester Prynne, and Ethan Brand: "To be sure, Twain is toying with the theme, evading final responsibility; for he knows that the most genteel post-Civil-War reader, secure in a world without slavery, will see Huck, not as a Satanic and hybristic rebel, setting the promptings of his own ignorant heart over the law of the land and the teaching of his church—but as a moral hero! Yet in Huck, for an instant at least, the marginal loafer, the uncommitted idler is revealed as the American Faust; the dark side turned up of what *Huckleberry Finn's* first reviewer called 'the ruffianism that is one result of the independence of Americans.' "[16]

Mark Twain himself experienced the loneliness of the wanderer, and it is worth considering briefly his transition from roving journalist and adventurer to married householder as a way of noting his personal reactions to life within the boundaries of the community. In the exclusive Nook Farm neighborhood of Hartford he built the grandest and most expensive house, entertained on a royal scale, and was the most imposing presence in a community that featured Harriet Beecher Stowe, Charles Dudley Warner, and Horace Bushnell. Though he clearly dominated this little world, his latest biographer points out that Mark Twain at the same time "achieved a remarkable degree of community and identification with his Nook Farm neighbors. For the first time since his boyhood in Hannibal he was part of the fabric of society, and although he turned a bitter eye on practically every American phenomenon of his time he rarely questioned his life in Hartford."[17] In Hartford Mark Twain enjoyed the fulfillment of the personal success he had desired—financial abundance, a wide and formidable reputation, and a dominant and secure place in a community whose genteel tastes in literature he strove deliberately and successfully to please. As Kenneth Andrews indicates, Mark Twain wrote *The Prince and The Pauper* in response to Nook Farm's desire that he turn his attention to what it considered serious literature, and that his objective and restrained treatment of society in *Huckleberry Finn* can be attributed to "his own brief equable arrangement with life" at Nook Farm.[18]

Whether the compromise resolutions of the "boy books" were shaped by Mark Twain's consciousness of the moral darkness beyond the community and by his own contentment within it, it does seem certain that the novels do in a sense duplicate his own "equable arrangement." It is in this sense that the four novels considered above are "fictions," books which stress and are flawed by an idealized notion of life. In Mark Twain's next novel he was unable to rely on fictional compromises to resolve the thematic conflicts. As we shall see, the irreconcilable realities of *A Connecticut Yankee* are at the heart of its chaotic structure and uncertain characterization.

CHAPTER TWO

A Connecticut Yankee: "Ah, What a Donkey I Was"

THE *Atlantic Monthly* in 1875 published Mark Twain's Mississippi reminiscences. Looking back from the landlocked perspective of middle age, he created the figure of the cub pilot, the feckless but sympathetic "boy," prototype of Tom Sawyer and Huck Finn. But Mark Twain himself was twenty-one years old when he commenced his river apprenticeship, and the image he constructs of the mature pilot in "Old Times on the Mississippi" is not so much wistful hyperbole as the epitome of an image of manhood he had cherished throughout his career as pilot, fortune hunter, and journalist in the 1850's and 1860's. "A pilot in those days," Mark Twain remembers, "was the only unfettered and entirely independent human being that lived in the earth. Kings are but the hampered servants of parliament and the people; parliaments sit in chains forged by their constituency; the editor of a newspaper cannot be independent, but must work with one hand tied behind him by party and patrons, and be content to utter only half or two-thirds of his mind; no clergyman is a free man and may speak the whole truth, regardless of his parish's opinions; writers of all kinds are manacled servants of the public. We write frankly and fearlessly, but then we 'modify' before we print. In truth, every man and woman and child has a master, and worries and frets in servitude; but, in the day I write of, the Mississippi pilot had *none* . . . here was the novelty of a king without a keeper, an absolute monarch who was absolute in sober truth and not by a fiction of words" (XII, 118–19).[1] As characterized by Captain Bixby in "Old Times," the pilot embodies all of the qualities requisite to the safe passage of a steamboat through tricky and dangerous waters. He is quick-minded, courageous, self-reliant, and strong-willed. But the most striking element in the quoted passage is the equation of the pilot's power with his independence. As Mark Twain warms to his task and expands the image, he ignores the fact that the pilot had independent control only over the operations of the vessel. What is stressed instead is his unparalleled independence and unlimited power—the "king without a keeper." However contrary to the kind of independence Huck Finn's adventures were to define, the notion of "absolute" authority was in fact central to the young writer's definition of independence. Most important, that image of the pilot—embodying Mark Twain's notions of manhood and of a man's relation to the world—was crucial not only to his personal criteria of success, but was significantly linked to his belief in modern man's superiority to his predecessors, to his faith in material and moral progress, and to his enthusiastic endorsement of aggressive leadership and modern technology. The eventual collapse of this vulnerable image would bear significantly upon his work as a writer, particularly upon his fifth novel. But up to the time he wrote *A Connecticut*

Yankee, and especially at the outset of his career, this image of manhood colored his view of himself and the world around him.

MARK Twain left Hannibal, Missouri, in 1853 at the age of seventeen, " 'wandering,' " his brother Orion wrote later, " 'in search of that comfort and that advancement and those rewards of industry he had failed to find where I was.' "² By 1862 he had been a printer in four cities, a steamboat pilot, and a fortune-hunting miner in Nevada and California. Early letters suggest a conception of himself as a man who takes naturally to authority. From New York he wrote in 1853, "if I don't manage to take care of *No. I,* be assured you will never know it. I am not afraid . . . I shall ask favors from no one, and endeavor to be (and shall be) as 'independent as a wood-sawyer's clerk.' "³ A few years later as a prosperous steamboat pilot he was anxious to assert his assumption of family leadership, though Orion—ten years his senior—was titular head. "When you want money," he wrote to his brother, "let Ma know, and she will send it. She and Pamela are always fussing about change, so I sent them a hundred and twenty quarters yesterday—fiddler's change enough till I get back, I reckon."⁴ In 1861 Orion became Secretary to the Territory of Nevada, and he financed his younger brother's mining expeditions. Nevertheless, Mark Twain wanted his mother to know that he himself was "at the helm. . . . I have convinced Orion that he hasn't business talent enough to carry on a peanut stand . . . if mines are to be bought or sold, or tunnels run, or shafts sunk, parties have to come to me—and me only. I'm the 'firm,' you know."⁵

As his career advanced, prestige and power were incorporated into Mark Twain's self-image. He was proud of his berth on the *City of Memphis* because it was paying handsomely in money and reputation: "the young pilots who used to tell me, patronizingly, that I could never learn the river cannot keep from showing a little of their chagrin at seeing me so far ahead of them. Permit me to 'blow my horn,' for I derive a *living* pleasure from these things."[6] In 1862, as Carson City correspondent for the Virginia City *Territorial Enterprise,* he considered himself to be something more than legislative reporter. "I was a mighty heavy wire-puller at the last Legislature," he boasted in one letter. "I passed every bill I worked for. . . . Oh, I tell you a reporter in the Legislature can swing more votes than any member of the body."[7]

Doubtless Henry Nash Smith's view that Mark Twain's boast was idle brag and no more is closer to the truth,[8] but it was apparently important for Mark Twain to feel that his position as journalist was influential. DeLancey Ferguson comments on Mark Twain's resistance to his mother's and sister's urgings that he return to the river when it was cleared for traffic in 1863: "He had tasted the power that lies in printer's ink, and the petty authority of a pilot over a handful of people on a steamboat had lost its allure."[9]

The *Enterprise* job marked the beginning of a career as a working journalist that took Mark Twain west to the Hawaiian Islands for the Sacramento *Union* in 1866 and east through Europe and the Holy Land for the San Francisco *Alta California* the following year. But the newspaper work provided him with an opportunity to expand his horizons in more than a geographical sense. As a writer he tended to praise those men who best exemplified his personal image of manhood. In particular, he evaluated public officials in terms of his notions of success and of the idea that the man who demonstrates the virtues of self-reliance can be expected to watch capably over the welfare of others. His published remarks on the leaders he encountered in his foreign travels indicate that the men who won his admiration were not only dedicated to political, material, and moral progress, they operated independent of and in opposition to outmoded tradition. Such men, in Mark Twain's mind, were dedicated to the people they led. No vague theorists, they had little respect for tradition; actively and enthusiastically they confronted the task of lifting their people into the nineteenth century. The first such men Mark Twain encountered on his travels who merited the right to guide the destinies of their people were the Protestant missionaries to Hawaii and the strong native King of the Islands.

His attitude toward the missionaries was not entirely favorable. He disliked them intensely for their narrow, doctrinaire puritanism, their lack of humane sympathies. Mark Twain mocked their religious parochialism, ironically lamenting the fate of those countless natives who died before the missionary help arrived and went "to their graves in this beautiful island and never knew there was a hell."[10] But this hint that the missionaries were really snakes in the Garden did not prevent Mark Twain from ardently singing their praises. Viewed from a different angle they were heroic bearers of civilization's light, "a band of stern, tenacious, unyielding, tireless, industrious, devoted, old Puritan knights . . . full of that fervent zeal and resistless determination inherited from their Pilgrim forefathers, [who] marched forth and seized upon this people with a grip of iron and infused into their being, wrought into their very natures, the spirit of democracy and the religious enthusiasm that animated themselves."[11] One is tempted to defend as intentional the implicit irony of the passage, but similar remarks lessen the probability. In Mark Twain's view the missionaries were wrenching the natives out of the past, from slavery toward self-determination and dignity. The missionaries, he wrote, have "clothed them, educated them, broken up the tyrannous authority of their chiefs, and given them freedom and the right to enjoy whatever the labor of their hand and brains produces, with equal laws for all alike who transgress them."[12] In short, Mark Twain congratulated the missionaries for confirming their own manhood by conferring it upon the natives.

Similarly, the powerful autocrat of the Islands earned Mark Twain's praise even as he contested with the missionaries for political dominance. Kamehameha V was an efficient exploiter of power for his people's welfare, or so Mark Twain argued. The King weakened the legislature and limited suffrage, but it mattered not to Mark Twain that these actions lessened the missionaries' political power as well as that of the people. Kamehameha had "very great power," Mark Twain wrote, "but he is a man of good sense and excellent education, and has an extended knowledge of business . . . therefore he uses his vast authority wisely and well."[13]

In Mark Twain's judgment, capable and responsible autocracy was preferable to inefficient democratic process. Witness his admiration of Captain Ned Blakeley and his qualified approval of a western desperado named Slade in *Roughing* It. Blakeley served as arresting officer, judge, and executioner of a man who murdered his first mate; and, although Mark Twain casts a comic tone over this recording of the incident, he juxtaposes the story with a denunciation of the jury system (IV, 67–75). Slade was hired by the Overland Stage Company to bring law and order to the stage route. In a short time he had "killed several of the worst desperadoes of the district, and gained such a dread ascendancy over the rest that they respected him, admired him, feared him, obeyed him!" (III, 66).

Mark Twain even more enthusiastically endorsed the absolute ruler of France, Napoleon III. In *The Innocents Abroad* he exploited the striking contrast presented by the Emperor and the Sultan of Turkey as the two chiefs of state reviewed troops on parade in Paris: "Napoleon III, the representative of the highest modern civilization; Abdul Aziz, the representative of a people by nature and training filthy, brutish, ignorant, unprogressive, superstitious—and a government whose Three Graces are Tyranny, Rapacity, Blood. Here in brilliant Paris, under this majestic Arch of Triumph, the First Century greets the Nineteenth." (I, 120). Abdul is dismissed as a degenerate wastrel of his enormous power, a slothful tyrant "who believes in gnomes and genii and the wild fables of the Arabian Nights, but has small regard for the mighty magicians of to-day, and is nervous in the presence of their mysterious railroads and steamboats and telegraphs" (I, 122). Napoleon, however, is in the best tradition of aggressive manhood. Once an outcast wanderer, he had "schemed and planned and pondered over future glory and future power," ultimately to be welcomed to it by "applauding armies" and the "thunders of cannon" (I, 121).[14] Mark Twain hailed him as a leader of "shrewd good sense" and "self-reliance," the emblem of "Energy, Persistence, Enterprise" (I, 155, 123).

Mark Twain's enthusiasm for aggressive leadership was matched by his indifference to the problems of its followers. Citing Napoleon's rebuilding program, he reported that hungry mobs would gather no more in the crooked lanes of Faubourg St. Antoine to breed rebellion and chaos. The Emperor is "building in their stead noble boulevards as straight as an arrow—avenues which a cannon-ball could traverse from end to end without meeting an obstruction more irresistible than the flesh and blood of men—boulevards whose stately edifices will never afford refuges and plotting places for starving, discontented revolution-breeders" (I, 154). Even so, Napoleon has taken care to guarantee a fair share of liberty along with material blessings, although not so much freedom as to cause inefficiency in the machinery of government. There is all the freedom one wants, "but no license . . . to interfere with anybody, or make any one uncomfortable" (I, 122–23).

Similar callousness is found scattered throughout his early writings. In his Hawaiian letters he noted that coolie laborers had replenished the declining native population, and he urged Californians to bring in the cheap and efficient Chinese labor, freeing the American laborer to engage in capitalistic enterprises.[15] In *The Innocents Abroad* he was less than sympathetic toward the poor and helpless. Natives of the Azores are "vermin," Moroccan women in Tangiers are "savages," Greeks, Turks, and Armenians are liars and cheats, and the Holy Land is populated with beggars: "old men and old women, boys and girls, the blind, the crazy, and the crippled, all in ragged, soiled, and scanty raiment, and all abject beggars by nature, instinct, and education" (II, 234). Natives of his own country fared no better. Writing in the *Galaxy* magazine in 1870 he complained that the plains Indian "is not rich enough to own a belt; he never owned a moccasin or wore a shoe in his life; and truly he is nothing but a poor, filthy, naked scurvy vagabond, whom to exterminate were a charity to the Creator's worthier insects and reptiles which he oppresses."[16] In *Roughing It* he characterized the Goshoots as representative of all Indian tribes—beggarly, vicious, slothful: "the Bushmen and our Goshoots are manifestly descended from the self-same gorilla, or kangaroo, or Norway rat, whichever animal-Adam the Darwinians trace them to" (III, 132).

Critics have variously explained the causes of Mark Twain's lack of perception and sympathy. Edgar M. Branch argues that Mark Twain readily sympathized with oppressed individuals but could not see that mass suffering was caused by the very forces he himself approved: "He instinctively sympathized with the more carefree Kanaka, burdened by Christian conversion with the qualms of conscience, the torture of remorse, and the knowledge of probable damnation; but he approved the activity that instilled these attitudes. He did not recognize, in other words, those human dispositions which he condemned, when they were formulated in terms of class and cultural relationships."[17]   Louis J. Budd attributes Twain's insensitivity to his zeal for nineteenth-century notions of progress and chides him for judging the "dirt, poverty, begging and endemic disease" he saw in Europe and the Holy Land "by the current gospel of success, blaming it either on laziness or lack of gusto for applied science."[18]   When Mark Twain wrote of men as beggars and thieves by instinct and training, of Indians as direct descendants of gorillas, he was in his own way finding them guilty of their unfortunate condition. Back of his contempt was the assumption that they were willfully lazy, superstitious, and ignorant, unwilling to be fully human, hence deserving their ignominy.

A belief that manhood was a matter of will and energy was a part of his general view. He was always ready to denounce those institutions and customs that seemed to restrain manhood, but at the same time he more forcefully pursued the theme of self-reliance and aggressive action as a solution to the problem. Therefore, he immediately responded to whoever demonstrated independence of thought and action. Despite his general contempt for the Hawaiian legislature he was quick to praise it for a momentary assertion of manhood. Mark Twain believed that first-rate men have no time to play games in a legislature while "their affairs go to ruin. . . . Few such men care a straw for the small-beer distinction one is able to achieve in such a place."[19] The only preventive against the enactment of idiotic law was the presence in the house of "a sensible man—a man of weight—a big gun," capable of ending silly debate with five sentences of common sense.[20] But on the day the finance minister forced his way into the speaker's chair and attempted to dominate the session "the poor humbled and brow-beaten country members threw off their fears for the moment and became men," forcing the official's withdrawal.[21]

Mark Twain again made his point, that self-assertion is the first step toward manhood, in *The Innocents Abroad*. He seemed to assume that the Florentine beggars could rise above their condition by striking directly at what he considered to be the root of their problem: " 'Oh, sons of classic Italy, *is* the spirit of enterprise, of self-reliance, of noble endeavor, utterly dead within ye? Curse your indolent worthlessness, why don't you rob your church?' " (I, 266). The joke is in earnest. The Church was an enemy of progress, but the solution was in the hands of those human beings it oppressed. Exercising a similar logic, Mark Twain railed against the Renaissance artists, protesting against "the grovelling spirit that could persuade [them] to prostitute their noble talents to the adulation of such monsters as the French, Venetian, and Florentine princes of two and three hundred years ago" (I, 268).

For Mark Twain the lesson is clear. Devotion to false gods results in human debasement, but direct action against the forces of tyranny implies an opposite, noble result. Aggressive, even violent action, is the answer to those forces which prevent man from becoming independent and fully human. The truly independent man stands on his own two feet and demonstrates his manhood in action, relying entirely upon himself.

In 1886 Mark Twain began work on a novel whose protagonist replaced the steamboat pilot as the epitome of manhood. In Hank Morgan he instilled the swagger of his own youthful self-assurance and all of the civilizing zeal of the Protestant missionaries. The Yankee even more enthusiastically applied the practical, progressive programs of a Louis Napoleon, and, sharing Mark Twain's assumption that manhood is as close as one's bootstraps, he took upon himself the transformation of a repressive totalitarian regime. Ultimately, the Yankee failed, as did the novel. Henry Nash Smith argues that in *A Connecticut Yankee* Mark Twain attempted to promote a modern civilization whose values he actually distrusted. "Mark Twain could not work out adequately this contrast of medieval and modern civilization because the protagonist who represented the modern world in the story was an inadequate vehicle for depicting industrial capitalism. In more metaphorical terms, the American Adam representing an older agrarian or pre-agrarian order could not be made into a Prometheus creating and administering an economic system comparable in complexity to the actual economic system of post-Civil War America."[22] My own view is that the thematic collapse of *A Connecticut Yankee* is caused not so much by a conflict of cultural values as by a conflict between Hank Morgan's humanitarian impulses and his destructive lust for power and adulation.

As I have attempted to show, before he came to his fifth novel Mark Twain held potentially conflicting views of the individual's relation to the community. One, characterized by the image of manhood that he promoted as journalist and travel writer, applauded the men who directly and aggressively dominated the community for its own good. Ideally, these heroes applied a combination of authoritarian leadership and modern technology within a "democratic" framework in the interest of moral and material progress. Manhood meant self-realization and implied a strong and beneficial link between the individual and the community. But, as we have seen, in the fiction of the 1870's and 1880's, Mark Twain viewed the individual's domination of the community with a more skeptical and even more fearful eye. He repeatedly made it clear that his protagonists' efforts to triumph over it had little or nothing to do with the community's welfare; indeed, they were often made at its expense. Although he was sympathetic to their attempts, he was unwilling to endorse them fully, for he was afraid that triumph ultimately led to moral isolation.

What is implied by the restoration of Mark Twain's heroes to the community in the earlier novels is even more clearly evident in *A Connecticut Yankee*. If in his previous fiction Mark Twain had worked out compromise resolutions which permitted triumph without alienation, in *A Connecticut Yankee* the protagonist breaks with the community, attempts to destroy it, and ends his life in isolation and despair. This happens despite the fact that Hank Morgan belongs to the aggressive tradition of Louis Napoleon and the Protestant missionaries; that he articulates many of Mark Twain's views on politics, religion, morality, history, and technology; that he was chosen by Mark Twain to bring proof of the nineteenth century's superiority to a mindless and spiritless antiquity.

Hank Morgan's failure to transform a sixth-century monarchy into a nineteenth-century republic was to be expected. For obvious reasons he could not be permitted to change the course of history. But his last act in old England is to destroy 25,000 lives, and we are thus led to inquire why Mark Twain ended the Yankee's career with an act that falls just short of genocide. My suggestion is that Mark Twain came to grips with but could not resolve an issue that in his nonfictional prose he had assumed did not exist and which he submerged under contrived resolutions in his previous novels: that is, whether the individual who is liberated by technology to exercise the inherent virtues of common sense, self-reliance, and courage on behalf of the community will choose to use his power humanely or will corrupt himself in pursuit of selfish aims.

Howard G. Baetzhold's study of the composition of *A Connecticut Yankee* indicates that Mark Twain wrote the book in three stages: the opening narrative frame and the first three chapters in 1886; chapters 4 through 20, excluding chapter 10, in 1887; chapter 10, the remaining twenty-four chapters, and the return to the frame—"A final P. S. by M. T."—in a sustained drive from July 1888 through mid-April or mid-May 1889.[23]

Despite the forebodings of despair and violence in Mark Twain's early projections for the novel, there is no reason to doubt Baetzhold when he says that even after the first stage was written "Twain was merely having fun with his subject."[24] Transported to the sixth century, the Hartford mechanic and factory foreman is taken prisoner and has time to note the comic simplicity of the natives before the manuscript breaks off.

In the second stage of composition Mark Twain quickly elevated his protagonist to a position of great power and at the same time deepened his characterization to reveal two sides of his personality. The Yankee's "circus side" is revealed in his rise from prisoner at the stake to King Arthur's right-hand man. By proving himself a gaudier and more successful magician than Merlin, the Yankee wins the adulation of the entire populace and a position of power second to none: "I was no shadow of a king; I was the substance; the king himself was the shadow" (XIV, 61).

What he plans to do with his power at this early stage is not altogether clear. At first he seems most concerned with the limitation of the fame he has achieved. His bitterness against the Roman Catholic Church is caused by the fact that it prevents him from receiving due homage. He is admired by the people, but rather as a kind of powerful animal than as a man of genuine rank (XIV, 64). The Yankee's first reference to the struggle which will dominate the third stage of the book is thus set forth in the context of his quarrel with an institution that will not allow him proper respect. "Before the day of the Church's supremacy in the world, men were men, and held their heads up, and had a man's pride and spirit and independence; and what of greatness and position a person got, he got mainly by achievement, not by birth. But then the Church came to the front . . . she preached (to the commoner) humility, obedience to superiors, the beauty of self-sacrifice . . . patience, meanness of spirit, non-resistance under oppression; and she introduced heritable ranks and aristocracies, and taught all the Christian popula-

tions of the earth to bow down to them and worship
them" (XIV, 65). But when the Yankee next speaks
of manhood it is in an entirely different context. Shortly
after he has attained power he embarks on the first
of his two tours through the English countryside. Viewing the pathetic condition of a tyrannized people, Hank
Morgan reveals his intention to work for their eventual
liberation. He thus rejects the "circus side" of his nature,
which impels him to launch an angry and bloody in-
surrection, in favor of gradual progress through education (XIV, 108). In keeping with this intention he frees
several prisoners from Morgan le Fay's dungeons and
sends the most promising candidates to his "Factory," a
school where he is transforming " 'groping and grubbing
automota into *men*' " (XIV, 147).

By the end of the second stage of composition, then,
the Yankee has referred to manhood in conflicting con-
texts. He is angered that he has not been granted the
reputation as a man that his power and position have
earned him. But as the observer of human suffering
he thinks of manhood as the prime necessity of a de-
humanized nation. His concern with manhood is carried
over into the final stage of composition, where it fully
emerges in what I take to be the central conflict in the
Yankee's character, a conflict that develops as once
again he travels through England, this time with King
Arthur.

The final stage of composition can be divided into
four parts: (1) the summary which became chapter
10; (2) Hank Morgan's and King Arthur's travels in-
cognito, including their fall into and rescue from
slavery; (3) the Battle of the Sand Belt and events
leading up to it; (4) "Final P. S. by M. T."—the Yankee
returned to the nineteenth century.

Professor Baetzhold has shown that Mark Twain found

he had insufficiently prepared his readers for the technological means of the Yankee's sensational exploits in the Valley of Holiness (chapters 22-24) or the presence of his officer's candidates in chapter 25.[25] Also, Mark Twain must have felt he should explain the source of his man-factories in more detail. Hence chaper 10, "The Beginnings of Civilization." There the Yankee summarizes his clandestine establishment of a nineteenth-century industrial empire in sixth-century England. But he also reveals an unsteady and disturbing attitude toward power. Remarking that "Unlimited power *is* the ideal thing when it is in safe hands," the Yankee rejects dictatorship on the grounds that it inevitably passes into unreliable hands (XIV, 78). As he continues to think on this matter he tends to associate power with violence and his own potential for initiating it. "My works showed what a despot could do with the resources of a kingdom at his command. Unsuspected by this dark land, I had the civilization of the nineteenth century booming under its very nose! It was fenced away from the public view, but there it was, a gigantic and unassailable fact—and to be heard from yet, if I lived and had luck. There it was, as sure a fact and as substantial a fact as any serene volcano standing innocent with its smokeless summit in the blue sky and giving no sign of the rising hell in its bowels. . . . I stood with one hand on the cock, so to speak, ready to turn it on and flood the midnight world with light at any moment" (XIV, 78–79). The language suggests that Hank Morgan may have thoughts of using his enormous power against the people rather than for them,[26] and as he travels with the King it becomes increasingly clear that this is the choice he will have to make.

By and large Hank Morgan is restricted to a passive

role in his second journey. The requirements of the
disguise which he and the King assume are that they
behave quietly and even humbly. Once again the
Yankee observes suffering, executions, oppression; it appears that his continued preoccupation with manhood
is an indication of his deepening response to the needs
of the nation. He does not miss his chance, for example,
to point out to King Arthur with heavy irony the commoner's mode of survival. For in order to venture
among his subjects the King must acquire the manners
of his disguise: " 'You must learn the trick,' " the
Yankee tells him; " 'you must imitate the trademarks
of poverty, misery, oppression, insult, and the other
several and common inhumanities that sap the man-
liness out of a man and make him a loyal and proper
and approved subject and a satisfaction to his masters' "
(XIV, 274–75). Many of the Yankee's problems on the
road are caused by the King's inability to master the
pose of obsequiousness, but Hank Morgan is concerned
with the problem on a more philosophical level.

He is amazed, for example, to find that the oppressed
are often more than willing to support their oppressors
in time of crisis, and he draws a parallel to the pre-Civil
War South, where poor whites rallied around the slaveholders out of loyalty to a system which degraded them
as much as it did the slaves. The only consoling aspect
of this pitiable condition, he thinks, is that the poor
whites actually hated the slaveholders deep down in
their hearts, which "showed that a man is at bottom a
man, after all" (XIV, 299). When he is provided with
an actual example of a peasant who admits he loathes
his master, the Yankee is ecstatic. "There it was, you
see. A man *is* a man at bottom. Whole ages of abuse
and oppression cannot crush the manhood clear out
of him. Whoever thinks it a mistake is himself mistaken.

Yes, there is plenty good enough material for a republic in the most degraded people that ever existed . . . if one could but force it out of its timid and suspicious privacy, to overthrow and trample in the mud any throne that ever was set up and any nobility that ever supported it" (XIV, 301).

But although the Yankee desires to make men out of slaves and sends likely prospects to his man-factory, he appears to lack sympathetic regard for a real man when he finds one. Hank Morgan and the King find lodging with a lowly freedman named Marco, who introduces them to a very prosperous blacksmith. Although the Yankee seems to enjoy Dowley's company, he commences upon an elaborate plan to humiliate him. Inviting the blacksmith to Marco's hut for a lavish meal, he plans to set him to talking about his rise in the world and then let the wind out of his sails. Dowley is all too willing to cooperate, but when he finishes his personal success story, the Yankee pays the astronomical cost of the banquet with a casual flourish, and "the blacksmith was a crushed man" (XIV, 320).

The Dowley incident marks the reemergence of the Yankee's circus side and at the same time helps bring it into clearer focus. This aspect of his character turns out to be something more than a love of gaudy showmanship and applause—a desire, instead, for personal power arising from triumphs over others. Shortly after he gains his reputation as superior magician and his position as King Arthur's chief administrator, the Yankee reflects upon the difference between the nineteenth and the sixth centuries in terms of opportunities for personal advancement: "Look at the opportunities here for a man of knowledge, brains, pluck, and enterprise to sail in and grow up with the country. The grandest field that ever was; and all my own; not a competitor; not a man who wasn't a baby to me in acquirements and capacities; whereas, what would I amount to in the twentieth century? I should be a foreman of a factory, that is about all; and could drag a seine down-street any day and catch a hundred better men than myself" (XIV, 60–61). Personal advancement is associated in the Yankee's mind with personal authority. For all his talk of raising the level of manhood by giving it an opportunity to develop, his personal desires are inimical to such a program. On the contrary, he responds most vigorously only to those men who threaten his own authoritarian identity. Just as earlier on he was unwilling to share the limelight with Merlin, whom he humiliated twice, he cannot now pass up the opportunity to put Dowley in a position subordinate to himself.

Even more revealing than the Dowley incident is the Yankee's envy of and competition with his traveling companion, the King. When they are captured and sold to a slave trader the Yankee is delighted that he himself is worth more money than Arthur. "Dear, dear," he reflects, "it only shows that there is nothing diviner about a king than there is about a tramp, after all. He is just a cheap and hollow artificiality when you don't know he is a king. But reveal his quality, and dear me it takes your very breath away to look at him" (XIV, 352). Yet Hank Morgan is conscious of the fact that the King is valued low as a slave because he refuses to act like one. Even after concentrated beatings his "spirit" remains untouched. Earlier, Hank Morgan admired Arthur's courage in the hut of a peasant stricken with smallpox, and now he comments: "The fact is, the king was a good deal more than a king, he was a man; and when a man is a man, you can't knock it out of him" (XIV, 355). As a progressive humanitarian Hank Morgan is opposed to monarchy, but by the end of their journey together he thoroughly envies the King. When Launcelot and his knights arrive just in time to prevent the Yankee and the King from hanging for the murder of their slavemaster, Hank Morgan is enthralled by the effect the revelation of Arthur's true identity has upon the mob: "it was fine to see that astonished multitude go down on their knees and beg their lives of the king they had just been deriding and insulting. And as he stood apart there, receiving this homage in rags, I thought to myself, well, really there *is* something peculiarly grand about the gait and bearing of a king, after all" (XIV, 382).

In *The Prince and The Pauper* Edward returns to London to take his rightful place as a responsible ruler of his land, which Tom Canty is delighted to abandon. Edward's travels among the people have taught him humanity and humility; the Yankee's have provided him with envious awareness of the grandeur of power and have revealed his own egotistic tendencies to humiliate those whose presence appears to challenge his manhood. The Yankee returns to Camelot, but not to take up his rightful place within the community. From this point forward his commitment is not to raising a nation of slaves to manhood, but to lowering it to its knees by extending the range and pressure of his personal power.

Upon his return the Yankee faces a duel over an old grudge with Sir Sagramore. He elevates the significance of the duel to what he calls a climactic battle between himself and the aristocracy as it is represented by its power-arm, knight errantry. The duel also serves an important thematic function in revealing Hank Morgan's motives as "Prometheus" to a primitive land. In the enemy side he includes Merlin, his old antagonist: "all the nation knew that this was not to be a duel be-

tween two mere men, so to speak, but a duel between
two mighty magicians; a duel not of muscle but of mind,
not of human skill but of super-human art and craft;
a final struggle for supremacy between the two master
enchanters of the age" (XIV, 385).

Merlin is the symbol of the power which ignorance
and superstition encourage. Every time the Yankee
defeats him—and he does so at intervals throughout—
we are meant to recognize the superiority of modern
practical knowledge over superstition and ignorance.
As the Yankee says after the tournament, "every time
the magic of fol-de-rol tried conclusions with the magic
of science, the magic of fol-de-rol got left" (XIV, 396).
Now whenever the Yankee works a "miracle"—such as
blowing up Merlin's tower with blasting powder or restoring the Holy Fountain with a few pieces of pipe,
a pump, and some firecrackers—it is clear that his success
depends on his technological knowledge. So far as the
sixth-century audience is concerned, however, Hank
Morgan's incantations, which he provides on each oc-
casion, are the source of his success. As he confesses,
"you can't throw too much style into a miracle. It costs
trouble, and work, and sometimes money; but it pays
in the end" (XIV, 213). Whether the Yankee or Merlin
wins the battles of the miracles can make no significant
difference from the audience's point of view. The crowds
will adore and fear whoever succeeds in astonishing
them most.

It is through his "miracles" that the Yankee early
gains enormous power. Further, his successes depend on
the same essential ingredient as Merlin's before the alien
steals his thunder—the ignorance of the audience. The
goal of each performance is to win its allegiance, more
accurately its subjection. Therefore Hank Morgan is
perfectly right to style himself as a magician, for his

methods and his intentions are no different than those of his arch-rival. His goal is to keep the masses in ignorance, consequently in fear of him. At the same time, performing miracles is a relatively harmless activity. The Yankee need hurt nothing but Merlin's ego while he indulges the benign aspect of his "circus side," his love of gaudy effect and applause. Further, it can be argued that the power he gains by the early miracles will be applied for the good of the nation he amazes with them.

But Hank Morgan wants more than applause. His travels with the King reveal his desire to assert his own manhood against other individuals, but in the contest with Merlin and the knights he attempts to assert it against the entire nation. To prove manhood he must defeat opponents less easily intimidated than the masses —the aristocracy and the Church. The so-called duel of minds is therefore ended in the Yankee's favor only after he kills a dozen knights with his revolvers. Violence and death mark the end of knight-errantry and begin what Hank Morgan calls "the march of civilization" (XIV, 396).

Having won the climactic battle he feels secure enough to unveil that hidden "volcano," his technological empire. Though he is still committed to an official policy of gradualism, he reveals also his deeper desire for control of the "republic": "I may as well confess, though I do feel ashamed when I think of it: I was beginning to have a base hankering to be its first president myself. Yes, there was more or less human nature in me; I found that out" (XIV, 400). Events provide him with the opportunity to put his urgings into action. Though he does not plan to institute universal suffrage and a representative government until the people are fully ready for them, the Church forces his hand. It tricks him into leaving the country, then takes advantage of a civil war between the knights to issue an Interdict and plunge the nation into darkness and confusion.

Again Hank Morgan demonstrates his readiness to assert his authority when threatened. He immediately takes up the Church's challenge and declares his republic thirty years earlier than planned. But the Church proves to be a more persuasive and powerful opponent than any of the Yankee's former antagonists; his reaction to the people's failure to respond to his proclamation is final proof of the extent of his selfishness. Violently disgusted at the populace's pledge of allegiance to the Establishment, he turns his technology against the nation. With dynamite, electric fences, Gatling guns, and flood waters the Yankee and his small force of well-trained boys wipe out 25,000 knights. At the same time he destroys his technological empire by detonating explosives planted in his factories: "I touched a button, and shook the bones of England loose from her spine!" (XIV, 433). Strangely, he considers this appalling violence in the same light as one of his benign miracles, a grand triumph which makes a deep impression on an audience: "This mighty victory," he announces, "stands without example in history. So long as the planets shall continue to move in their orbits, the BATTLE OF THE SAND-BELT will not perish out of the memories of men" (XIV, 435).

Hank Morgan wins the battle but loses the war. With his small army he is trapped in a circle of rotting corpses. Merlin again appears and for once performs a successful miracle. The Yankee is put into a thirteen-century sleep. But the important question is why Mark Twain ended the Yankee's career in an insane act which destroys both himself and his enemies. I suggest that the answer lies in Mark Twain's disenchantment both with a world incapable of reform and with the motives of his protagonist.

If Mark Twain was uncertain about the direction of this novel when he began writing, he made revealing if somewhat misleading statements about its meaning when he had finished. In the main he seemed to think of the book as a revolutionary document for the common man.[27] As to the lesson itself, he told his London publishers that the novel was directed to English readers in particular and was an effort "to pry up the English nation to a little higher level of manhood."[28] In other letters he suggested that the way to manhood lay in violent action against tyranny. To one correspondent he pointed out that his Yankee's proclamation of a republic was remarkably similar to the document which "proclaims the Republic of the United States of Brazil."[29] In a letter to William Dean Howells he endorsed the French Revolution as "next to the 4th of July & its results . . . the noblest & the holiest thing & the most precious that ever happened in this earth."[30] In 1890 he wrote to the editor of *Free Russia* protesting that modifications of the Czarist monarchy fell short of necessity. Equating the Czar with a "bloody-jawed maniac," he saw nothing to do but destroy him. "Of course," he said, "I know that the properest way to demolish the Russian throne would be by revolution. But it is not possible to get up a revolution there; so the only thing left to do, apparently, is to keep the throne vacant by dynamite until a day when candidates shall decline with thanks. Then organize the Republic."[31]

These letters immediately following the completion and publication of the novel tend to support Smith's view that Mark Twain increasingly identified himself with his narrator as the action gathered momentum.[32] Combined with the violence of the ending and the comments Mark Twain made on the finished novel, it can plausibly be argued that he came to believe change could be brought about only by destructive action against oppressors. At the same time there is sufficient evidence to suggest that the Yankee's final resort to violence is impelled by his recognition, shared by Mark Twain, that earlier assumptions were no longer valid. Hank Morgan began his career in England on the same assumptions Mark Twain held in his journalism, that is, that a strong leader with faith in technology and a belief in progress can benefit the community. The Yankee assumed, as Mark Twain did, that the community would cooperate with progressive leadership in the interest of its own welfare. Hank Morgan is careful to point out to his squeamish boys that only "nobles and gentry" will be killed in the battle, but the explosive destruction also symbolizes his frustrated rage at the victims of the aristocracy who choose to remain forever "sheep" and "human muck": "Ah, what a donkey I was! Toward the end of the week I began to get this large and disenchanting fact through my head: that the mass of the nation had swung their caps and shouted for the republic for about one day, and there an end! The Church, the nobles, and the gentry then turned one grand, all-disapproving frown upon them and shriveled them into sheep! . . . Imagine such human muck as this; conceive of this folly!" (XIV, 429–30). When the Yankee goes into battle and blows up his civilization, Mark Twain is also exploding his hope that "civilization" may change propensities so deeply ingrained.

Still, I doubt that Mark Twain fully identified himself with his protagonist in this crisis. In all probability, Mark Twain was aiming his bombs and machine guns at an even larger target than a corrupt community; if he raged with the Yankee against a world incapable of regeneration, his violent anger was also directed against the Yankee for his inability to rise above "human nature."

We have seen that Mark Twain associated technology with human progress. Louis Napoleon used it to confer material blessings and civil order on France, but Abdul Aziz remained a barbaric tyrant because he had "small regard for the mighty magicians of to-day." To Mark Twain, technology performed miracles in liberating men from material and moral poverty. Thus if the Yankee calls himself a magician, his creator had sound reason for initially supporting his use of the term. Because he has the power of technical knowledge to change a world, Hank Morgan is a magician in a more real sense than his use of Merlin's tricks would suggest. It has been argued that Mark Twain associated machinery with magic because despite his "interest in gadgets and machines . . . he did not really understand what the experts were doing. . . . The technological feats that Mark Twain ascribes to his protagonist had not entered deeply enough into his experience to be fully grasped by his imagination."[33] Although Mark Twain may not have thoroughly grasped the workings of machinery, he did tend to view technology as the key ingredient in the performance of real miracles.

But though he assumed that man's machines were proof of his capacity to improve his condition, he was forced to an opposite conclusion in *A Connecticut Yankee.* The "magic of science" is supposed to liberate an oppressed people; instead, the magician of science cannot rise above his selfish desires for adulation and power. He is not essentially interested in making men out of slaves, but in making them *his* slaves. Bent on transforming the world for his own purposes he becomes at the end an ominous symbol of "modern technological man. When he is through exercising his weapons, there will be even less of civilization than there was before he began his wonder-working transformation."[34] The machine makes dreams come true, but the Yankee dreams only for himself.

AT THE end of his book Tom Sawyer discovers not only a treasure in the cave, but the cave itself. Its hidden entrance makes it the perfect hideout for his projected robber gang. The novel ends at that point, but in a sense Hank Morgan's Battle of the Sand-Belt is Tom Sawyer's last stand. When the Yankee retreats to Merlin's Cave, there to direct the cataclysm that destroys his enemies and himself, we are witnessing the demented fulfillment of the ending of *Tom Sawyer*. In Hank Morgan Tom Sawyer's aggressive tendencies grow up unchecked, to erupt and obliterate not only human life, but Mark Twain's idealized relation of the individual and the community.

Despite its unchecked violence, reflecting a highly ambiguous and chaotic resolution, the ending of *A Connecticut Yankee* is in an ironic way appropriate to the meaning of the book. For the first time, Mark Twain did not employ the fictions that resolved his previous novels. Instead, he faced the reality he had to this point evaded—the fate of the individual who asserts himself against the community. Even the concluding chapter—"A Final P. S. by M. T."—underlines Mark Twain's rejection of his own fictional illusions. The reader accepts Hank Morgan's journey through time as impelled by Merlin's enchantment; but one wonders why the dying Hank Morgan now so closely identifies himself with a wife who has functioned chiefly as comic vehicle, and with the knights who have been his enemies. In his deathbed delirium he believes that the man sitting by his bed is his wife and that his projection forward in time is a nightmare in which he dreams he is a " 'stranger and forlorn in that strange England, with an abyss of thirteen centuries yawning between me and you! between me . . . and all that is dear to me, all that could make life worth the living!' " (XIV, 449). Because of these contrivances that set the final scene, Mark Twain's point is made clear: the Yankee is now an alien in the nineteenth century, isolated by time and event from any sense of his relation to the community. The age of industrial energy, whose technology and ethic was the source of his power, now represents the immensity of his loss. It has become an alien world from which his only refuge is identification with the medieval community he had abandoned and destroyed. Thus his futile refuge in illusion.

CHAPTER THREE

The Yankee as Old Man

IT MAY seem strange that the man whose energies were directed to transforming the medieval world is now so closely identified with it. But with one critical difference the end of *A Connecticut Yankee* is consistent with the pattern of Mark Twain's previous novels, that is, the restoration of the individual to the community he had attempted to dominate. The difference is that Hank Morgan cannot take refuge in a real community, but in an illusion that brings him a small measure of peace. Nevertheless, the illusion does not erase the fact that he is in the end a stranger, isolated and lost.

The novel's final scene indicates one of Mark Twain's two responses to his recognition that man cannot rise above his destructive compulsion to satisfy himself at the expense of his humanity. When he made his protagonist a victim and withdrew him from reality into the shelter of illusion, Mark Twain acknowledged that man needs illusion because the truth of his condition is too terrible to endure. This response suggests that Mark Twain's fear for the individual who becomes separated from the community had not diminished. If anything, it had increased now that the community was no longer morally suitable as a refuge. At bottom, Mark Twain had come to feel, the human being was weak, selfish, cruel, and petty. Man's happiness depended upon a vain belief that his life had dignity and meaning in the eyes of others. He was incapable of living anything but a lie and thus needed the comfort of the illusion.

At the same time, in the years following *A Connecticut Yankee,* the vindictive and outraged Hank Morgan would reappear in various guises to continue his cynical diatribes against a world incapable of regeneration. Before *A Connecticut Yankee* Mark Twain's fictional protagonists had been lively and imaginative children engaged in conflict with the town. In the after years he tended to depend upon knowledgeable men as narrative voices, men who looked upon the community from the authoritative perspective of age and experience. Their purpose was not only to hold the community responsible for its inhumanity, but more especially to explode the idealistic presumptions of youth, to present the community to them as a destructive force lacking dignity and love, unworthy of their confidence. As we shall see, Mark Twain's ambivalent attitude toward man's illusions is reflected in his use of the old man, who functions in the late fiction as exploder of illusions and victimizer of those who need their illusions to survive.

Mark Twain's use of old men involved a reworking of certain comic poses he had exploited for humorous purposes in the early travel literature and humorous sketches. Sometimes, according to John Gerber, he "pretended undue superiority . . . in posing as . . . the Instructor and the Moralist."[1] Now the point of view was much less a pretense and the element of humor disappeared. If in the past he had used the Instructor for "boisterous idiocy" and the Moralist to "make fun of such things as moralism itself,"[2] he now employed the Tutor to teach the uninitiated the disheartening truth about the world they lived in and trusted.

The outlines of Mark Twain's new fictional strategy and purpose appear in *The American Claimant,* published three years after *A Connecticut Yankee.* The Earl of Rossmore has upon his hands a recalcitrant son and heir who wishes "'to retire from what to me is a false existence, a false position, and begin my life over again . . . on the level of mere manhood, unassisted by factitious aids, and succeed or fail by pure merit or the want of it'" (XV, 6). The Earl is contemptuous of the lower orders and disdainful of his son's noble resolve. But he has the sense to let him strike out on his own in America and learn from experience: "'Let us see what equality and hard times can effect for the mental health of a brain-sick young British Lord. Going to renounce his lordship and be a man! Yas!'" (XV, 9).

The Earl is right to let his son go. Though it lacks the terrifying dimensions of the Yankee's adventures in sixth-century England, Berkeley's American sojourn teaches him that the manly virtues of self-reliance and equality have no relevance in the nation that virtually invented them.[3] The Yankee had been stymied by the people's adoration of nobility and rank; the Viscount finds in a land where titles do not exist that the same kind of self-destructive snobbery flourishes. His original expectations of a society welded by common humanity and progressive purposes are temporarily buoyed up by a Mechanics Club lecturer who proclaims the absence in America of "'misplaced reverence'" for cruel and arbitrary institutions (XV, 81). But he soon learns through experience that the spirit of humanity has not taken the place of cruelty. He witnesses the humiliation of a boardinghouse tenant who cannot pay his rent and is told by a cynical workingman friend that he should not expect too much from "human nature," that people naturally look down upon the man who loses his job and can no longer support himself. " 'Don't you know,' " Barrow says, " 'that the wounded deer is always attacked and killed .by its companions and friends?' " (XV, 108). Himself the victim of a sneering landlord when his money runs out, the Viscount concludes that "in a republic where all are free and equal prosperity and position constitute *rank*" (XV, 110).

Berkeley's decision to return home and resume his title is an indictment of American society. He has learned to his amazement that Barrow would gladly abandon his democratic principles and join the aristocracy if opportunity offered. Barrow argues that one might as well take advantage of a sham that an entire nation supports. As Berkeley interprets Barrow, " 'You have no blame for the lucky few who naturally decline to vacate the pleasant nest they were born into; you only despise the all-powerful and stupid mass of the nation for allowing the nest to exist' " (XV, 130). On the basis of his American education Berkeley reports to his father "that on the whole he had arrived at the conclusion that he could not reform the world single-handed, and was willing to retire from the conflict . . . to return home and resume his position and be content with it and thankful for it for the future, leaving further experiment of a missionary sort to other young people needing the chastening and quelling persuasions of experience, the only logic sure to convince a diseased imagination and restore it to rugged health" (XV, 214).

There can be no mistaking the ironic parallels between the Yankee's journey to England and the young aristocrat's pilgrimage to America. The Yankee assumed that modern machinery might lead to a revolution in human values. He did not realize that his technology could dazzle the nation but not make the slightest dent in its beliefs or effect a change in its responses to authority. Berkeley is astounded to find that a modern, progressive nation still responds to arbitrary authority. He comes to America to live free of pretense but learns that the world will have to be changed to conform to the frank and open principles of the idealist. The Viscount, however, is no revolutionary. Fortunately for his sanity, he has the advantage of sensible though cynical tutelage. His father has permitted him to learn by experience, and Barrow sets forth a realistic alternative to a pursuit that could result in despair and possibly in madness. The point of view of the cynical aristocrat and the resigned American prevail finally over the naive and youthful presumptions of the idealist.

Personal Recollections of Joan of Arc is also a kind of requiem for idealism and an object lesson in the hopelessness of individual effort against the community's cruel indifference. Joan, under divine mandate, is to deliver France from its oppressors, but her efforts are consistently betrayed by Church, King, and the French people. DeLancey Ferguson attributes much of the book's artistic failure to the lack of irreverent burlesque and less than vigorous depiction of medieval battle scenes,[4] but if we can view the story's narrator as Tutor it becomes clear that humor and vigor are not to be expected from a man whose purpose is to set forth the futility of individual effort. The Sieur Louis de Conte is eighty-two years old when he presents his disillusioning lesson for children. From the perspective of fifty years he specifically addresses his message to his "great-great-grand nephews and nieces" (XVII, vii). He enthusiastically recounts Joan's military triumphs but is clearly more interested in telling the story of how she was sold out by a feckless king, driven to distraction by the clergy, and abandoned by the people. Joan, who "rose above the limitations and infirmities of our human nature," was nevertheless betrayed by it (XVIII, 230). This is the lesson that he learned firsthand and now passes on to his youthful readers. De Conte notes that he was shocked when Joan was betrayed to the English but explains, "We were young, you see, and did not know the human race" (XVIII, 112). And later he explains his fallacious hope that the people would come to Joan's rescue at Rouen on the same grounds: "we were young, then; yes, we were very young" (XVIII, 256).

The Earl of Rossmore, Barrow, and the Sieur de Conte teach by appeals to experience what a more vigorous Tutor was to teach his student through theory. *What Is Man?*[5] is a dialogue between a Young Man who believes in man's "dignities, grandeurs, sublimities" (XXVI, 76) and an Old Man who proves that man is but a "machine," an "impersonal engine" (XXVI, 5). But it is essentially as moralist that the Old Man applies his law to the several pretensions of the human race. The Young Man, for example, believes in self-sacrifice; the Old Man cites the case of Alexander Hamilton, who "treacherously deserted [his family] and threw his life away, ungenerously leaving them to lifelong sorrow in order that he might stand well with a foolish world" (XXVI, 17). The Young Man claims man is the animals' superior because he has the "Moral Sense"; the Old Man says, "the fact that man knows right from wrong proves his *intellectual* superiority to other creatures; but the fact that he can *do* wrong proves his *moral* inferiority to any creatures that *cannot*" (XXVI, 89).

The Old Man's analysis shows that man is not free, that his thoughts and deeds are determined by outside forces. Granted that, moral judgments are irrelevant and pointless. But as moralist Mark Twain wants to hold man responsible for his constitutional inability to satisfy anybody but himself. It is this desire that makes the Old Man's lesson somewhat confusing and leads him into such inconsistent statements as the following: "The mind can freely *select, choose, point out* the right and just [course of action]—its function stops there. . . . It has no authority to say that the right one shall be acted upon and the wrong one discarded. That authority is . . . in the machine which stands for him" (XXVI, 91).

In three works, then, Mark Twain employed the Tutor-Pupil relationship to explode youthful notions that there is such a thing as self-determination. And in each case the Tutor shares the Yankee's contemptuous view of the community. The same pattern is repeated in the published version of the most famous of Mark Twain's late works, *The Mysterious Stranger*.[6] Satan appears to his pupils as a "youth" although he is actually 16,000 years old and possesses an intellect infinitely superior to the minds of his students. He teaches the same lesson the Old Man taught the Young Man, but Satan is a moralist as well as an instructor, and the determinism he serves up is part of his attack on man's pride in a life which has no more dignity and worth than a gnat's.

The attack on the community is more direct and dramatic than in *What Is Man?* Satan teaches his first lesson with a shocking example of his contempt. Out of mud he creates a tiny village, and the boys are mortified when he casually kills some of the inhabitants for offending him with their noisy squabblings. When, finally, he wipes out the entire population the boys burst into tears of horror. " 'Don't cry,' Satan said, 'they were of no value' " (XXVII, 21). The human race, Satan

points out, is a race of " 'sheep,' " each of which desires
above all else " 'to stand well in his neighbor's eye' "
(XXVII, 118). Theodor, the story's narrator, learns his
lesson well. He remembers Eseldorf as a town where
people were afraid of knowledge, where he himself
participated with the majority in cruel and arbitrary
persecutions because he was afraid a generous and
" 'manly' " act would get him in trouble (XXVII, 4, 65).

There are certain clear parallels between Satan in
Eseldorf and Hank Morgan in sixth-century England.
Both characters are projected into medieval communities,
and both possess greater knowledge than the people
they dazzle with extraordinary stunts. Both tangle with
lesser magicians, the Yankee with Merlin, Satan with
the wicked astrologer, and both withdraw from the time
and place in the end. One difference between the Yankee
and Satan is that the latter comes to Eseldorf to expose
man, whereas Hank Morgan acquires hopes of reforming
him, proposing as his model the democratic-technological
world of the nineteenth century. When Satan looks to
the future he shows Theodor the nineteenth century or
its equivalent, wherein technological advances serve
man's inhumanity: "He showed us slaughters more
terrible in their destruction of life, more devastating in
their engines of war, than any we had seen" (XXVII, 110).
Hank Morgan's optimism is only temporary, however,
and his final view of the community is identical with
Satan's. The Yankee reviles the people for their failure
to see clearly the truth of their condition; Satan says the
human race "lived a life of continuous and uninterrupted
self-deception. It duped itself from cradle to grave
with shams and delusions which it mistook for realities,
and this made its entire life a sham" (XXVII, 131).

Mark Twain's sympathy with the Old Man's point of
view is reflected also in his treatment of the boys who

appear in his late work, boys who share the detached and
cynical perspective. Bernard DeVoto's contention that
Theodor and his friends in *The Mysterious Stranger* are
reincarnations of Tom and Huck is an exaggeration.[7]
Before they are reconciled to it Tom and Huck do
violence to the community. Tom dupes it, Huck violates
its moral law, and both win free temporarily from its
restraints. Mark Twain's sympathies were basically with
the boys, but he treated the community as an entity made
up of human beings. He could mock the sentimentality
of the town in *Tom Sawyer*, yet the reader also senses
the genuine quality of the emotion as the " 'sold' " congregation sings out its gratitude and relief for the safe
return of the boys. In *Huckleberry Finn* the community
is portrayed as contemptible and dangerous, but because
of Huck's acute sympathy the reader reacts to the cruelty
and hypocrisy he witnesses with a similar kind of
sympathy for his fellow human beings.

Theodor is capable of sympathy in *The Mysterious
Stranger*, but his point of view is not permitted to prevail. Thus, when the boy calls torture "a brutal thing,"
Satan instructs him on the proper angle of vision, point-
ing out that torture is actually a " 'human thing,' " just
another example of the moral sense in action and proof
that man is inferior to the four-legged beasts (XXVII, 50).
Theodor differs from the boy-heroes of the 1870's and
1880's in another important sense: he never makes the
slightest effort to violate community standards or to
upset its peace of mind. On the contrary, he is completely intimidated by the town. From time to time
he does manage to escape its confines, but only to
accompany Satan on journeys through time and space.
Further, these are educational tours, the Tutor taking
his pupil on field trips to witness the limitless brutality
of man. Theodor's function is mainly to report the

examples he sees of the "weakness and triviality of our race" (XXVII, 136).

Theodor's and Satan's cosmic rambles are reminiscent of the journey that Tom, Huck, and ex-slave Jim take in *Tom Sawyer Abroad.* Instead of direct and lively involvements with the communities they sought to dominate or escape in the earlier novels, Jim and the two boys drift over the Sahara Desert, finding at one stopping place the bones and relics of a luckless caravan and witnessing from the air the destruction of another by a sandstorm. There is a hint of the earlier Huck's humanity in his eulogy of the devastated community (XIX, 94), but in the main he now functions dully as narrator of a tedious journey and as straight man for Jim and Tom. Tom, too, has changed. He seems older, with a broader, cynical knowledge of the world. He compares man to the flea, for example, elaborately holding forth on the proposition that the flea is actually the most intelligent and the strongest creature on the earth (XIX, 53–57). He explains to Huck what an import duty is: " 'a big tax, which they call a duty because it's their duty to bust you if they can' " (XIX, 98). Huck inquires whether in international relations an offending country always apologizes to the offended country. " 'Yes,' " Tom answers, " 'the little one does' " (XIX, 110).

In a limited way, then, even Tom performs here as one of Mark Twain's Tutors, but the important point is that the perspective is no longer that of a boy involved in a conflict with the community. His knowledge and his pronouncements are fitted instead to the dreary, blighted world that the Sahara symbolizes. He has become in *Tom Sawyer Abroad* one of Mark Twain's cynical protagonists. Mark Twain himself could no longer see the world through a boy's eyes. Instead, a wise and bitter old man looks out over the community with icy contempt. Satan, the Sieur de Conte, the Old Man, and the Earl of Rossmore share in varying degrees the knowledge that Hank Morgan died with, and they take pains to teach this knowledge to the young people who may otherwise believe in man's worth. They show their pupils that the community is contemptible because it does not permit freedom of action, virtuous conduct, manly effort; and Tom Sawyer finally sees it as Mark Twain did: a desolate place, devoid of joy and life.

B U T Mark Twain's attitude toward man's illusions was by no means unequivocal. The ambiguous role of the Old Man in *The Tragedy of Pudd'nhead Wilson* and "The Man That Corrupted Hadleyburg" suggests a sympathetic response to those for whom reality is the enemy of survival. The Old Man appears in Mark Twain's last major novel and his best late short story not only as a moralizing discoverer of human weakness, but as a victimizer who destroys at the cost of human life the illusions that sustain it.

The antagonists in *Pudd'nhead Wilson* are Roxana, a slave woman who lives on illusion, and David Wilson, who insists upon knowing and telling the truth. Roxy is one-sixteenth Negro; her son, fathered by a white aristocrat, is thirty-one thirty-seconds white and the exact double of Thomas à Becket Driscoll, born at the time of Roxy's son's birth to her master and his wife.[8] Soon after her son is born Roxy decides to kill him and herself rather than risk the chance that he will one day be sold into more arduous slavery on a downriver plantation. But on a sudden inspiration she switches the two babies in their cradles, dooming Thomas à Becket to a life of slavery and freeing her son—or so she believes —into the white community.

Roxy makes this decision in the mistaken belief that his new role will not cause his separation from her. For despite the fact that Roxy knows who her enemy is, she identifies herself with it, taking great pride in her whiteness and her white aristocratic heritage. Early in the novel she chides a fellow slave when he claims he is going to court her: " '*You* is, you black mudcat! . . . I got somep'n' better to do den 'sociat'n' wid niggers as black as you is' " (XVI, 10). Later, when she reveals to "Tom" the true nature of his heritage, she tells him his white father " 'wuz the highest quality in dis whole town' " (XVI, 75). She traces her ancestry back to Captain John Smith and lays the blame for her son's refusal to fight a duel in defense of the Driscoll honor on " 'de nigger in you. . . . Thirty-one parts o' you is white, en on'y one part nigger, en dat po' little one part is yo' *soul* " (XVI, 123).

Roxy decides to switch the babies after she prepares herself for death. Unwilling to have her body discovered in rags, she put on her best garment, "took off her handkerchief-turban and dressed her glossy wealth of hair 'like white folks' "; then she dressed her son in his white counterpart's finery (XVI, 19–20). At that moment she sees the alternative to suicide. Her decision originates in her identification with "white folks" and is carried through in the illusory belief that the cradle-switch does not imply a severance of the mother-son relationship. Roxy believes she is restoring her son to the white community of which she thinks she is a member.

Of course, she knows that more is involved than a change of clothes and names. For her deception to succeed she must treat her son with all the indulgence due a white master. But the necessity of deceiving the world very soon causes Roxy to be her own victim: "deceptions intended solely for others gradually grew practically into self-deception as well; the mock reverence became real reverence, the mock obsequiousness real obsequiousness, the mock homage real homage; the little counterfeit rift of separation between imitation slave and imitation master widened and widened, and became an abyss, and a very real one—and on one side of it stood Roxy, the dupe of her own deceptions, and on the other stood her child, no longer a usurper to her, but her accepted and recognized master, and her deity all in one, and in her worship of him she forgot who she was and what he had been" (XVI, 28–29).

Roxy's benevolent deception is a failure, for her urge to place her son within the white community leads to disaster. As a white aristocrat he is freed only to exercise a destructive temperament. Like Hank Morgan before him, "Tom" is given the opportunity to destroy others and ultimately himself. From infancy he becomes increasingly selfish, brutal, and violent. His progress is inexorable from liar to gambler, to thief, to murderer. His antisocial exploits lead to his exposure as a slave; in the end he is sold down the river, meeting the fate that Roxy in the beginning had tried to prevent.

Through it all Roxy remains the victim of her twin illusions, that Tom's position in the white social structure of Dawson's Landing can be made permanent and that he will be grateful to her for what she has done. For fifteen years after his birth she endures his contempt. Then, freed by Percy Driscoll's will, she works for eight years on a steamboat until a rheumatic condition forces her retirement. When she applies for aid and comfort to the boy who had used her so badly he indifferently rebuffs her, and in hurt and anger she reveals her true

relationship to him. But Roxy responds to her deeper
need for love and proposes a radical plan to get him out
of his current dilemma. "Tom" has been burglarizing
Dawson's Landing homes to pay off his gambling debts;
so Roxy suggests that he sell her into slavery, pay off
his creditors, and eventually buy her freedom. "Tom"
is astounded, but Roxy explains that " 'Dey ain't nothin'
a white mother won't do for her chile. . . . In de inside,
mothers is all de same.' " Her reward will be his
gratitude, " 'all de pay a body kin want in dis worl', en
it's mo' den enough' " (XVI, 143).

But "Tom" betrays her. She has assumed he will sell
her to an upcountry farm; he sells her instead to an
Arkansas cotton-planter: "so poor Roxy was entirely
deceived; and easily, for she was not dreaming that her
own son could be guilty of treason to a mother who . . .
was making a sacrifice for him compared with which
death would have been a poor and commonplace one"
(XVI, 145). It is significant that Roxy associates real
slavery with downriver plantations. The image of plantation darkies sweating under the overseer's whip promotes
in her and her fellow upcountry Negroes the belief that
their condition is by comparison fortunate and that
they are hardly slaves at all. But for her son to treat
her as a Negro and sell her down the river—that is a
revelation too stupendous to be borne. Unable to bear
the abuse she suffers in Arkansas, Roxy escapes and returns to Dawson's Landing, where she learns that "Tom"
has been in contact with her master and has agreed to
recapture her for him.

One illusion is now completely dispelled, the belief
that her son would return his mother's love. In response
she exerts punitive pressure, threatening to expose him
unless he confesses his faults and requests of the judge
the money to buy her freedom. Knowing that such a

confession is likely to cost him his inheritance, "Tom" resolves not to confess to his guardian, but to rob him, and when the Judge catches him in the act he stabs him to death.

Thus, Roxy destroys everything she has lived for. Her attempts to preserve her and her son's identification with the white community end in their destruction. When she learns at the trial that "Tom" is a murderer and that Pudd'nhead Wilson has discovered his true parentage, she collapses: "Roxy's heart was broken . . . the spirit in her eye was quenched, her martial bearing departed with it, and the voice of her laughter ceased in the land" (XVI, 202). Roxy's illusion ends, and yet illusion is necessary for her survival. When it is destroyed, her spirit dies.

Ironically, however, Roxy's tragic commitment to self-deception is the one real link she has with the white community. For the white citizens of Dawson's Landing also depend on self-deception for the preservation of their values and way of life. This fact is powerfully dramatized in the strange career of the man responsible for Tom's exposure and Roxy's spiritual death.

David Wilson seems to be one of Mark Twain's authoritative characters, typical in the late period of his fiction. An intellectual, he is interested "in every new thing that was born into the universe of ideas" (XVI, 9). Specifically, he is intrigued by the new science of finger-printing. Over the years he collects the fingerprints of all the villagers. As he explains, a fingerprint is a man's "'physiological autograph'"; he cannot counterfeit it, "'nor can he disguise it or hide it away, nor can it become illegible by the wear and mutations of time'" (XVI, 192). His fingerprint collection provides him with a certain quality of knowledge common to Mark Twain's old men, not to mention a certain amount of power.

It is through the fingerprints that he exposes "Tom" as murderer and slave. In addition, Wilson is an ironist and a cynic. In fact, his ironic detachment is what causes the label of "Pudd'nhead" to be attached to him. When his ironical aphorisms are passed among the towns-people they are convinced he is a "pudd'nhead": "irony was not for those people; their mental vision was not focused for it" (XVI, 40).

But Mark Twain said he thought of Wilson not "as a *character*, but only as a piece of machinery."[9] The remark is apt; although Mark Twain provided Wilson with all of the attributes of his Old Man, he actually employed him as the community's representative, opposed to Roxy and "Tom." Despite his apparent intellectual and moral detachment from the town, Wilson symbolizes its angle of vision. It appears that he is a pariah, but he fits into the community better than the villagers think at the time of his arrival. Despite his interest in ideas and his cynical aphorisms, he never substantially challenges the values of the community, and in time he is accepted by Dawson's Landing as something more than an entertaining speculator in vague and useless notions. After twenty-three years in the town he is asked to run for mayor; after he wins the election, he caps his triumph by clearing a visiting Italian nobleman of the murder and proving that "Tom" Driscoll did it. It is as mayor, or town spokesman, that he seeks and fetches the truth that finishes "Tom" and Roxy, and it is in this role that Wilson functions as a piece of machinery. Not only does he officially represent the community, he sees with its angle of vision. He began his career in the town as a pariah because he was an ironist, but he triumphs ultimately because it turns out that irony is not for him either.

One of the occupations Wilson tries in his early days

is accounting, and in a sense he functions as the town's accountant at the trial, that is, one who impartially and mechanically straightens out the books. After "Tom" is exposed, the Judge's creditors argue that he is their property and should be sold to help pay off the Judge's debts. Further, they claim, "Tom" is in a sense not guilty. If his identity had been discovered earlier he could have been sold, thus preventing the murder of the Judge; "therefore it was not he that had really committed the murder, the guilt lay with the erroneous inventory. Everybody saw that there was reason in this. Everybody granted that if 'Tom' were white and free it would be unquestionably right to punish him—it would be no loss to anybody; but to shut up a valuable slave for life—that was quite another matter" (XVI, 203).

It has been suggested that Wilson's courtroom revelation of "Tom's" genealogy "demonstrates that the official culture, with its vaunted ideals of honor and chivalry and ancient lineage, is merely a facade for deceit, avarice, and illegitimacy."[10] But for the town itself there is no revelation, because the community is incapable of fully applying the disclosures made at the trial. Wilson is the town's hero because he has put things back in their proper places. To the town there is a clear distinction between black and white, even if the black is thirty-one thirty-seconds white. Dawson's Landing cannot learn by experience and is incapable of recognizing its fallibility. Wilson is a piece of the machinery, the town is the machine, capable of thinking and acting only along certain prescribed lines.

Leslie Fiedler claims that the detective-story motif requires Wilson to restore order to the community and to restore himself to it in the process. Even so, he continues, "there remains beneath the assertions that man is master of his fate, the melancholy conviction that to be born is to be doomed, a kind of secularized Calvinism."[11] The doom of which Fiedler speaks is, I think, man's very existence, made small and mean by a lack of humane vision. This is the important theme of the novel that Wilson's presence dramatizes. Roxy must cling to her illusion in order to preserve her identity. The irony is that the illusion to which she clings is of a relationship based on mutual love and devotion. But opposed to her is the white community and its spokesman, David Wilson—a community whose very existence depends on preservation of illusion, but of another sort. Their illusion of white purity precludes humane values. Roxy needs the community in order to survive, but it is a community which, seen through, makes life not worth living.

The same impossible tension exists in "The Man That Corrupted Hadleyburg," a story that contains another of Mark Twain's cynical characters to promote an official thesis. Mark Twain employs in the story a shadowy figure, "a bitter man and vengeful," to expose the moral dry rot of the community and to teach its smug, self-righteous citizens a lesson. But this thesis is undercut by Mark Twain's deeper concern with the necessity and futility of illusion.

Hadleyburg is scarcely different from every other small town, except that over the years it has built up a widespread reputation for uprightness and honesty. The town is so proud of its renown, "and so anxious to insure its perpetuation, that it began to teach the principles of honest dealings to its babies in the cradle. . . . Also, throughout the formative years temptations were kept out of the way of the young people, so that their honesty could have every chance to harden and solidify, and become a part of their very bone" (XXIII, 1). The vengeful stranger, once gratuitously hurt by one of the townspeople, designs an elaborate strategy to reveal the hollowness of the town's honesty by exposing its nineteen principal citizens as liars and hypocrites. He forces each of them to lie in order to claim a sack of gold, and at the public meeting where the exposure takes place he also reveals his own intentions: "'I wanted to damage every man in the place, and every woman—and not in their bodies or in their estate, but in their vanity—the place where feeble and foolish people are most vulnerable. . . . Why, you simple creatures, the weakest of all weak things is a virtue which has not been tested in the fire'" (XXIII, 52–53). In the end the town appears to have learned its lesson, for it subsequently changes its name and revises its motto from "Lead Us Not Into Temptation" to "Lead Us Into Temptation (XXIII, 69). For this reason critics tend to treat the story as an affirmative document. Pascal Covici, Jr., for example, says that in "welcoming temptation, the townspeople show both their acceptance of the sinful nature of men and their readiness to assume the existential dignity which humanity attains by exercising the power of choice that only the acceptance of evil can posit."[12]

But I doubt that the story's overt moral and the stranger's stern sermonizing should be so implicitly trusted. First, it should be noted that the focal characters, Edward and Mary Richards, are a part of the group of nineteen principal citizens who represent Hadleyburg's hypocrisy and greed, but that they differ markedly from the others. Titles attached to identified members of the group suggest that Mark Twain had in mind Hadleyburg's most important citizens: Wilson the lawyer, Pinkerton the banker, Deacon Billson, "Dr." Harkness. Yet Edward Richards, at whose home the moralizing stranger leaves the fake bag of gold and instructions for its distribution, is a mere wage-slave at Pinkerton's bank.

The reader first encounters him at the end of a long day, "'tired clear out,'" complaining of his long hours as "'another man's slave, and he sitting home in his slippers, rich and comfortable'" (XXIII, 5). When the opportunity to escape the poverty which has crippled their lives arises, the Richardses leap quickly to the bait. When they decide to put in a false claim they also face the fact that their vaunted honesty is no shield against temptation. As Mrs. Richards puts it: "'it is my belief that this town's honesty is as rotten as mine is; as rotten as yours is. . . . There, now, I've made confession, and I feel better; I am a humbug, and I've been one all my life, without knowing it. Let no man call me honest again—I will not have it'" (XXIII, 15–16). Her husband endorses the indictment; but for the Richardses it is one thing to discard illusion and quite another to live with the truth.

At the public meeting where the gold is to be given to the rightful claimant it soon is apparent that a gigantic hoax has been played. The lawyer Wilson and Deacon Billson are the first members of the nineteen to be exposed. They attempt to bluster and lie their way out of false positions, but Richards, anticipating exposure and ridicule, decides to confess. His attempt at genuine honesty is balked, however, by what appears to be an unconscious conspiracy of the assembled townsfolk. They had been joyously deriding the exposed hypocrites, yet their treatment of Richards indicates their need for a symbol of honesty. They shout him down with cheers of praise when he rises to confess, and the Reverend Burgess, believing himself in Richards's debt for a previous favor, now suppresses the incriminating claim. Once again the hapless clerk tries to confess when the assemblage decides to auction off the sack of lead and donate it to the town's only incorruptible man. But intimidated by the tumult of the bidding and restrained by his wife's pathetic murmur—" 'we are so poor' "—he "sat still; sat with a conscience which was not satisfied, but which was overpowered by circumstances" (XXIII, 55–56). Even the avenging stranger is shocked by Richards's apparent incorruptibility, and he arranges for the couple to receive a fortune of $40,000.

With their reputations perfectly secure and a fortune in their grasp, the old couple appear to have gained everything their commitment to dishonesty was designed to gain. But they cannot live with the knowledge of what they are. Their guilty consciences quickly lead to paranoid delusions. Richards imagines that Burgess is actually perpetuating a plot to revenge himself for a wrong Richards did him in the past. The old couple see signs of conspiracy in meaningless incidents and quickly fall into delirium. Just before they die Richards burns the money, confesses his guilt, but also makes a final accusation—that Burgess had set a trap for him. "Burgess's impassioned protestations fell upon deaf ears; the dying man passed away without knowing that once more he had done poor Burgess a wrong" (XXIII, 68).

In one critic's view, the suffering and death of the Richardses is not in vain, for they have profited from it. "Experience," Clinton Burhans says, "has made Richards's conscience a highly complex faculty in which moral perception and direction and the motivating emotion of self-approval work together to produce real honesty."[13] Honesty is scarcely the entire issue. What is at stake in the pathetic story of the Richardses is the necessity of illusion to survival. When the old people believed in their honesty they were at least able to function. Their lives were mean and petty, though not entirely lacking in virtue and a measure of contentment. But after his fall the bank clerk could no longer trust himself to " 'let

oceans of people's money pour through my hands' "
(XXIII, 60). His and his wife's self-recognition may
have been the first step toward moral awakening, but
it left their lives devoid of happiness. "Richards and his
old wife sat apart in their little parlor—miserable and
thinking. This was become their evening habit now:
the lifelong habit which had preceded it, of reading,
knitting, and contented chat, or receiving or paying
neighborly calls, was dead and gone and forgotten"
(XXIII, 20–21). Worse, their recognition that they are
hypocritical members of a hypocritical community has
the effect of making them feel like pariahs. When the
town praises their honesty they feel that they are the
only dishonest people in Hadleyburg. Surely their
delusion about Burgess indicates their desire to be exposed and punished by the community from which, they
feel, they have morally alienated themselves.

The Richardses' experience serves no useful moral
purpose. Their realistic appraisal of their own and
Hadleyburg's moral culpability sets them apart from
the community and destroys them. Further, a reformed
Richards does no more good in the world than a weak
and hypocritical one. As moral coward he had abetted
the persecution of Burgess by his failure to speak out
on behalf of a man falsely accused of a crime. As reformed man, armed with moral perception, he speaks
out and again puts Burgess in a false and dangerous
position.

HUCKLEBERRY Finn considered himself a moral pariah
because he found himself unable to capitulate to the
values of the community. But he had in addition to a
conscience the courage of his instinct, which moved him
to violate the very standards he accepted. The Rich-

ardses, on the other hand, cannot survive beyond the town's limits. What little happiness they have in life depends entirely on capitulation to Hadleyburg's values and Hadleyburg's illusion. Old and weak, they lack the strength to free themselves from the community which the story condemns. Like Roxy, they can survive only by sharing its illusion. When the illusion is destroyed, life is finished. The trouble is that reality impinges upon the dream. Hence, the enigmatic stranger is not so much the moralist as he is victimizer, insisting upon truth at the expense of frail human life.[14] In his disillusionment following *A Connecticut Yankee* Mark Twain excoriated the community from a detached and cynical point of view. But the Old Man is finally the discoverer of the darkest truth of all, the truth of man's pathetic inability to survive self-knowledge.

NOTES

CHAPTER ONE

1 *The Writings of Mark Twain,* Definitive Edition, ed. Albert Bigelow Paine (37 vols.; New York, 1922–1925), V, 75. Future references to this edition by volume and page number are given parenthetically in the text.

2 "On the Structure of *Tom Sawyer,*" *Modern Philology,* XXXVII (Aug. 1939), 84–85.

3 Albert E. Stone, Jr., *The Innocent Eye: Childhood in Mark Twain's Imagination* (New Haven, 1961), pp. 79–80.

4 Blair, "On the Structure of *Tom Sawyer,*" p. 88. Robert Regan, who has also noticed the "theatrical artificiality" of the town, accepts Blair's thesis but argues that Tom in the final chapter is "a relapsed juvenile" whose major goal is leadership of the other boys. See *Unpromising Heroes: Mark Twain and His Characters* (Berkeley and Los Angeles, 1966), pp. 126–30.

5 Regan, *Unpromising Heroes,* p. 149.

6 *Mark Twain: The Development of a Writer* (Cambridge, Mass., 1962), p. 132.

7 *Ibid.,* p. 134.

8 Quoted in Hamlin L. Hill, "The Composition and the Structure of *Tom Sawyer,*" *American Literature,* XXXII (Jan. 1961), 386.

9 *Ibid.,* p. 387.

10 *Ibid.,* p. 388.

11 Leo Marx, "Mr. Eliot, Mr. Trilling, and *Huckleberry Finn,*" *The American Scholar,* XXII (Autumn 1953), 426–27.

12 *Ibid.,* p. 440.

13 As Henry Nash Smith defines the term, "the overlayer of prejudice and false valuation imposed upon all members of society in the name of religion, morality, law, and culture" in his introduction to the Riverside Press edition of *Adventures of Huckleberry Finn* (Boston, 1958), p. xvi.

14 Charles Crowe, "Mark Twain's *Huckleberry Finn* and the

American Journey," *Archiv für das Studium der Neuren Sprachen und Literaturen,"* (Aug. 1962), pp. 149–50.

15 William R. Manierre, " 'No Money for to Buy the Outfit': *Huckleberry Finn* Again," *Modern Fiction Studies,* X (Winter 1964–65), 342.

16Leslie A. Fiedler, *Love and Death in the American Novel* (New York, 1960), p. 578.

17 Justin Kaplan, *Mr. Clemens and Mark Twain* (New York, 1966), p. 141.

18 *Nook Farm: Mark Twain's Hartford Circle* (Cambridge, Mass., 1950), pp. 188–98, 215.

CHAPTER TWO

1 The original series of articles forms chaps. 4–17 of *Life on the Mississippi.*

2 Quoted in A. B. Paine, *Mark Twain, A Biography: The Personal and Literary Life of Samuel Langhorne Clemens* (3 vols.; New York, 1912), I, 93.

3 *Mark Twain's Letters,* ed. A. B. Paine (2 vols.; New York, 1917), I, 24. Hereinafter cited as *Letters.*

4 *Ibid.,* p. 51.

5 *Ibid.,* p. 67.

6 *Ibid.,* p. 43.

7 Quoted in *Mark Twain of the Enterprise,* ed. Henry Nash Smith (Berkeley and Los Angeles, 1957), p. 13.

8 *Ibid.,* p. 15.

9 DeLancey Ferguson, *Mark Twain: Man and Legend* (Indianapolis and New York, 1943), p. 86.

10 Walter Francis Frear, *Mark Twain and Hawaii* (Chicago, 1947), p. 331. Frear reprints the twenty-five letters to the Sacramento *Union,* hereinafter cited as *Sandwich Islands Correspondence.*

11 *Ibid.,* p. 353.

12 *Ibid.,* p. 289.

13 *Ibid.,* p. 319.

14 Interesting in this regard is the almost unquestionable fact that Mark Twain fictionalized Louis Napoleon's rags-to-riches ascent, as Robert Regan points out in *Unpromising Heroes,* pp. 70–74.

15 *Sandwich Islands Correspondence,* p. 406.

16 *Contributions to the Galaxy: 1868–1871,* ed. Bruce R. Mc-Elderry, Jr. (Gainesville, 1961), p. 71.

17 Edgar M. Branch, *The Literary Apprenticeship of Mark Twain* (Urbana, 1950), p. 181.

18 Louis J. Budd, *Mark Twain: Social Philosopher* (Bloomington, 1962), p. 12.

19 *Sandwich Islands Correspondence*, p. 320.

20 *Ibid.*, p. 321.

21 *Ibid.*, p. 319.

22 *Mark Twain's Fable of Progress: Political and Economic Ideas in "A Connecticut Yankee"* (New Brunswick, N. J., 1964), p. 104.

23 "The Course of Composition of *A Connecticut Yankee:* A Reinterpretation," *American Literature*, XXXIII (May 1961), 195–214.

24 *Ibid.*, p. 198.

25 *Ibid.*, p. 211.

26 Allen Guttman has noted the conflict between the Yankee's professed belief in democracy and his fascination with power, in "Mark Twain's *Connecticut Yankee:* Affirmation of the Vernacular Tradition?" *New England Quarterly*, XXXIII (June 1960), 232–37.

27 *Letters*, II, 527–28.

28 *Ibid.*, p. 525.

29 *Ibid.*, p. 520.

30 *Mark Twain–Howells Letters: The Correspondence of Samuel L. Clemens and William D. Howells, 1872–1910*, ed. Henry Nash Smith and William M. Gibson (2 vols.; Cambridge, Mass., 1960), p. 613.

31 *Letters*, II, 537.

32 Smith, *Mark Twain's Fable of Progress*, pp. 54–55.

33 *Ibid.*, p. 88.

34 Charles S. Holmes, "*A Connecticut Yankee in King Arthur's Court:* Mark Twain's Fable of Uncertainty," *South Atlantic Quarterly*, LXI (Autumn 1962), 470.

Chapter Three

1 John C. Gerber, "Mark Twain's Use of the Comic Pose," *PMLA*, LXXVII (June 1962), 297.

2 *Ibid.*, p. 299.

3 Roger B. Salomon has noted similar parallels between *A Connecticut Yankee* and *The American Claimant*, in *Twain and the Image of History* (New Haven, 1961), pp. 127–32.

4 *Mark Twain: Man and Legend*, pp. 260–61.

5 *What Is Man?* was published in 1906, but it germinated over

a long period of time, from as early as 1882. See Alexander E. Jones, "Mark Twain and the Determinism of *What Is Man?*" *American Literature,* XXIX (March 1957), 2–3.

6 John S. Tuckey's textual study of *The Mysterious Stranger* shows that the final "dream ending" chapter was not intended for the version of the story to which it was posthumously attached. Tuckey shows that Mark Twain worked on the "Eseldorf" version off and on between 1897 and 1900, that the ending of the published story actually belongs to another version, which Mark Twain worked on between 1902 and 1908. See *Mark Twain and Little Satan: The Writing of "The Mysterious Stranger"* (West Lafayette, Ind., 1963).

7 *Mark Twain at Work* (Cambridge, Mass., 1942), p. 128.

8 The true Thomas à Becket Driscoll is the son of Percy Northumberland Driscoll and his wife. Valet de Chambre, the slave boy whom Roxy substitutes for Thomas à Becket, is born to Roxy and Colonel Cecil Burleigh Essex, a white aristocrat who does not figure in the story. When the boys are fifteen years old Percy Driscoll dies and "Tom" becomes the ward of Judge York Leicester Driscoll, Percy's brother. But as Henry Nash Smith points out, "from the standpoint of imaginative coherence Judge York Leicester Driscoll is the father of Tom just as clearly as Roxy is his mother." See *Mark Twain: Development of a Writer,* p. 174.

9 *The Love Letters of Mark Twain,* ed. Dixon Wecter (New York, 1949), p. 291.

10 Smith, *Mark Twain: The Development of a Writer,* p. 182.

11 Leslie A. Fiedler, "As Free as Any Cretur . . .," *New Republic,* CXXXIII (Aug. 22, 1955), 17. Reprinted in *Mark Twain: A Collection of Critical Essays,* ed. Henry Nash Smith (Englewood Cliffs, N. J., 1963), p. 137.

12 *Mark Twain's Humor: The Image of a World* (Dallas, 1962), p. 203. See also Paul J. Carter, "Mark Twain: Moralist in Disguise," *University of Colorado Studies in Language and Literature,* VI (Jan. 1957), 74.

13 Clinton S. Burhans, Jr., "The Sober Affirmation of Mark Twain's Hadleyburg," *American Literature,* XXXIV (Nov. 1962), 383.

14 James M. Cox cites Hank Morgan, David Wilson, the Mysterious Stranger, and the man that corrupted Hadleyburg as intruders bent on "disturbing the peace." See "*A Connecticut Yankee in King Arthur's Court:* The Machinery of Self-Preservation," *Yale Review,* L (Autumn 1960), 101–102.

INDEX